Teaching Towards Green Schools

This engaging and timely book showcases practical ways that PreK–12 teachers and school leaders can create and implement sustainability-focused projects and practices in their classrooms and schools, helping promote a healthy, sustainable environment and curriculum for students and leading the way towards becoming a green school.

Sharing real-world case studies and detailed walk-throughs of sustainable schools in action – from Madison, Alabama, to Bali, Indonesia – author Linda H. Plevyak lays out the benefits, principles and practices of creating a sustainable school from beginner classroom projects like creating a garden, recycling and composting to more complex and school-wide initiatives like energy audits, creating an environmental management system, engaging with policy and building and leveraging community partnerships. Plevyak highlights sustainable practices that can be developed with little to no budget and focuses on those that support the development of critical thinking skills, promote project-based learning and consider the environment as a learning tool, incorporating sustainability as a natural progression of the learning process.

The book outlines extensive resources teachers and schools can use to embed sustainability in their programs and curriculum, offering teachers, school leaders and policy makers the tools they need to provide this generation of students with the knowledge and skills to create a more sustainable world.

Linda H. Plevyak is Graduate Director of the School of Education and Associate Professor of Curriculum and Instruction at the University of Cincinnati, U.S./

T0383670

Also Available from Routledge Eye On Education
(www.routledge.com/k-12)

Teaching Climate Change for Grades 6–12
Kelley T. Le

*STEM Road Map 2.0: A Framework for Integrated
STEM Education in the Innovation Age*
Carla C. Johnson, Erin E. Peters-Burton,
and Tamara J. Moore (eds.)

*Ask, Explore, Write! An Inquiry-Driven
Approach to Science and Literacy Learning*
Troy Hicks, Jeremy Hyler, and Wiline Pangle

Rigor in the 6–12 Math and Science Classroom: A Teacher Toolkit
Barbara R. Blackburn and Abbigail Armstrong

*Teaching Science Thinking: Using Scientific Reasoning
in the Classroom*
Christopher Moore

*Getting Started with STEAM: Practical Strategies
for the K – 8 Classroom*
Billy Krakower and Meredith Martin

STEM Road Map Curriculum series
Carla C. Johnson, Janet B. Walton, and Erin E. Peters-Burton (eds.)
Co-published with NSTA Press:
Rebuilding the Natural Environment, Grade 10
Mineral Resources, Grade 11
Our Changing Environment, Grade K
Formation of the Earth, Grade 9
Genetically Modified Organisms, Grade 7

Teaching Towards Green Schools

Transforming K–12 Education through Sustainable Practices

Linda H. Plevyak

Routledge
Taylor & Francis Group

NEW YORK AND LONDON

Cover image: © Getty images

First published 2022
by Routledge
605 Third Avenue, New York, NY 10158

and by Routledge
4 Park Square, Milton Park, Abingdon, Oxon, OX14 4RN

Routledge is an imprint of the Taylor & Francis Group, an informa business

Library of Congress Cataloging-in-Publication Data
A catalog record for this book has been requested

ISBN: 978-0-367-75908-7 (hbk)
ISBN: 978-0-367-75907-0 (pbk)
ISBN: 978-1-003-16452-4 (ebk)

DOI: 10.4324/9781003164524

Typeset in Palatino
by Apex CoVantage, LLC

Access the Support Material: www.routledge.com/9780367759070

To my husband, Howard, you are my best friend and I can't imagine life without you (though Bella runs a close second).

To my parents, Carl (aka Bert) and Carol, for your love, support and guidance (you are great traveling and drinking partners).

To my sister, Laurie, and brother, Carl, you both are amazing (your spouses are pretty darn special too).

To all those who read this book, thank you for your dedication in creating green schools.

Contents

List of Illustrations . . . . *xii*
Meet the Author . . . . *xiii*
Preface . . . . *xiv*
Acknowledgments . . . . *xvi*

1 **Introduction to Green Schools** 1
   Vignette 1
   Chapter Objectives 2
   Green School Movement 2
   The Emergence of Green Schools 3
   Connection to Environmental Education and
   Sustainability 7
   Green Schools and the Organizations That Influence
   and Support Them 10
      Eco-Schools 11
      Center for Green Schools 11
      Green Schools Alliance 12
      Green Schools Initiative 13
      Green Schools National Network 13
      International School Grounds Alliance and Green
      Schoolyards America 13
      Green Strides 14
      Institute for the Built Environment 14
      National Green Schools Society 15
   Conclusions 15
   Questions to Consider 16

2 **Whole School Framework and the Green Ribbon
   Award** 19
   Vignette 19
   Chapter Objectives 20

The Green Ribbon Award and the Three Pillars of
Sustainability 20
Using the *Whole School Sustainability Framework*
(WSSF) as a Roadmap to Create a Sustainable School 22
 Vision and Mission Alignment 24
 Interdepartmental Learning. 25
 Catalytic Communication 26
 Charismatic Champions. 26
 Engaging and Active Design 27
 Progressive Efficiency. 28
 Healthy Systems 28
 Connection to Place. 28
 Student Powered 29
 Longevity 31
 Finances 31
Creating a Green School and How Interconnectedness
Can Be Achieved 32
Conclusions 34
Questions to Consider. 35

3 **Getting Started in Creating a Green School** **37**
Vignette 37
Chapter Objectives 38
Green Schools and the Connection to Quality Education 38
 Benefits to Teaching and Learning 39
 Improvement to Human Health and Wellness 41
School Location: Development and Use of Green Space 43
Step-by-Step Process of Greening a School 46
Team Building 54
Conclusions 57
Questions to Consider. 57

4 **What Does a Successful Green School Look Like?** **62**
Vignette 62
Chapter Objectives 63
Creating the Ideal Environment for Learning. 63
Characteristics of a Green School 66

Physical Plant 66
Health and Wellness 67
Curriculum 69
The Use of Outdoor Space 70
How Leadership Can Support the Development
and Success of a Green School 72
Conclusions 74
Questions to Consider 75

5 Teaching Project- and Problem-Based Learning
   in a Green School 79
Vignette 79
Chapter Objectives 80
Teaching in a Green School 80
Integrating Inquiry and Problem-Based Learning
with Green School Practices 91
Student-Centered, Experiential Learning 98
Conclusions 100
Questions to Consider 101

6 The Management, Aesthetics and Efficiency
   of a Green School 106
Vignette 106
Chapter Objectives 107
Green School: Plant Management, Physical Health
and Improved Performance and Aesthetic/School
Environment 107
Plant Management 110
Physical Health and Improved Performance 112
Aesthetic/School Environment 115
Environmental School Audits 117
Energy-Efficient Systems and Sustainable
Practices 118
Development of Environmental Management
That Supports Sustainability 121
Conclusions 122
Questions to Consider 123

7 **Policy, Safety and Diversity, Equity and Inclusion Within a Green School**. **129**
Vignette. 129
Chapter Objectives 130
Government, Policy, Non-profits and Green Schools. 130
    Government and Policy 130
    Impact of Non-profits. 134
Green School Safety and Supervision Considerations. 136
    Outdoor Areas. 136
    Supervision. 139
Diversity, Equity and Inclusion and Green Schools. 139
Conclusions 143
Questions to Consider. 143

8 **Cost Benefits of Green Schools and How to Leverage Funding and Partnerships**. **146**
Vignette. 146
Chapter Objectives 147
Cost Benefits of Green Schools 147
Grant Funding and How to Stretch a Budget 153
    Grants and Resources. 154
Partnerships That Can Support Green School Projects 155
Low- or No-Cost Ways to Be Sustainable. 157
    Energy. 160
    Water. 160
    Safe Materials and Healthy Air. .160
Green Schools and the Impact on the Local Community . . . 160
    Green Schools Create Jobs 163
Conclusions 164
Questions to Consider. 164

9 **How to Evaluate Campus, Curriculum and Community Sustainability Initiatives** **167**
Vignette. 167
Chapter Objectives 168
Green School Evaluation: What Is It and How
Can It Be Used? 168

What Is Evaluation? 169
What Type of Evaluation Should Be Used?. 170
Evaluating the Interconnection of Sustainability
Initiatives. 172
The Evaluation Process for Both Course- and
Campus-Based Sustainability Initiatives 177
    Evaluation of Course-Based Sustainability
    Initiatives 177
    Evaluation of Campus-Based Sustainability
    Initiatives 180
    Grant Writing and Funding. 183
Evaluation of Community Relationships to Keep
Them Healthy and Meaningful. 186
Conclusions 188
Questions to Consider. 189

Additional Resources 191

Illustrations

Figures

1.1 Eco-Schools seven-step process. 5
2.1 WSSF, Center for Green Schools (2014) 23
2.2 Transdisciplinary approach to learning 25
3.1 Green Schools step-by-step approach 55
5.1 Willingham's Simple Memory model 81
5.2 An experiential learning approach. 99
9.1 Interconnectedness of sustainability initiatives 178

Tables

8.1 Financial benefits of building a green school 148
8.2 How a green school could obtain funding for
    renewable energy 155
9.1 Project Evaluation Toolbox 173
9.2 Example rubric for the Roosevelt case study 182
9.3 Example timeline for the Roosevelt Garden Project. 184

Meet the Author

Linda H. Plevyak is the graduate director of the School of Education and associate professor of Curriculum and Instruction at the University of Cincinnati. She has served as a member of the University of Cincinnati, Ohio (U.S.A.) faculty since 2000. She oversees the PhD and master's programs and is interested in school service that is focused on sustainability and environmental education. Her research interests include the development of green schools based on the three-pillar framework of reducing environmental impact, improving health and wellness and offering effective environmental-sustainability education. Dr. Plevyak is married, lives in Cincinnati, OH (Over-the-Rhine) and has a dog, Bella, who is likely lying by her side right now.

Preface

This book is a culmination of years of talking and learning about sustainability and green schools. My research with numerous schools around the world has helped me to better understand what is required to create a green school. In 2018, I interviewed teachers and administrators in the United States about how their schools achieved the Green Ribbon Award (ED-GRS) through the U.S. Department of Education. From these interviews, it was clear that it takes a team of dedicated people to create a successful green school. I followed up with more interviews in 2020 and 2021 with other Green Ribbon Award winners as well as international schools that received Eco-School Green Flag Awards or followed the United Nations Sustainable Development Goals. Some of these schools have been following sustainability practices for decades, and others for just a few years. You will see these case studies interspersed throughout the book, highlighting their creativity and amazing efforts in relation to sustainability.

Chapter 1 discusses the emergence of green schools and highlights some of the non-profit organizations that influence and support sustainability in PreK–12 education. Chapter 2 focuses on the Whole School Sustainability Framework as a process to create a green school. The U.S. Green Ribbon Award and the three pillars of sustainability are also discussed in Chapter 2. Chapter 3 emphasizes the benefits of teaching and learning and health and wellness of a green school as well as the step-by-step process in creating a green school. Chapter 4 shares what a successful green school looks like, including creating the ideal environment for learning, characteristics of a green school, use of outdoor space and how leadership can support the development of green schools.

Chapter 5 highlights and discusses project- and problem-based learning in a green school while emphasizing student-centered, experiential learning. Chapter 6 goes into detail about plant management, physical health and improved performance within a green school. It also shares information about environmental school audits and energy efficient systems. Chapter 7 goes over policy, safety and diversity, equity and inclusion information that relates to a green school. Chapter 8 discusses cost benefits of green schools, grant funding, how to stretch a budget, partnerships that support green school projects, low- or no-cost ways to be sustainable and the impact of a green school on the local community. Chapter 9 shares ways to evaluate campus, curriculum and community sustainability initiatives. This last chapter also explains the evaluation process and includes a simulated case study that provides example evaluations.

Acknowledgments

Thank you to all of the teachers and administrators in the green schools around the world who were willing to take time to talk with me about their amazing work. You all are an inspiration.

Thank you to my friends and family for asking about the book and giving me encouragement; it meant a lot.

Thank you to Simon Jacobs and AnnaMary Goodall at Routledge; you both were incredibly helpful and supportive.

Thank you to Heather Jarrow at Routledge for getting this project started. Your efforts are greatly appreciated.

Thank you to the University of Cincinnati, which allows faculty to take a sabbatical to focus on research. Without that dedicated time, this book would have taken a lot longer to write.

1

Introduction to Green Schools

"I don't want to protect the environment. I want to create a world where the environment does not need protecting."

Unknown

Vignette

What do you imagine when you think of a green school? Is there a lot of natural light, plenty of warm paint tones, solar panels on the roof and classrooms with hydroponic plants and a farm-to-table cafeteria? These schools exist and are likely even more amazing than what you imagined. One such place, North Park School for Innovation in Columbia Heights, MN captures all parking lot and playground runoff in rain gardens populated with native pollinator plants. They have also planted hundreds of trees, bushes and pollinating plants throughout the school's property and recently acquired a biodigester to turn their food scraps, milk cartons and paper towels into compost for their garden and plants.

DOI: 10.4324/9781003164524-1

Chapter Objectives

- ◆ Discuss the evolution of green schools.
- ◆ Focus on historical aspects of environmental education (EE), sustainability and their connection to green schools.

Green School Movement

Approximately 56.4 million students spend five days a week in a school building (National Center for Education Statistics, 2020). If you add public school employees, including teachers and staff members (6.7 million), there are 63.1 million people working or learning in U.S. K–12 schools, which equates to almost 20% of the U.S. population (IBISWorld, 2020; National Center for Education Statistics, 2020). It makes sense that schools should be a place that focuses on the social, emotional and physical health of those who spend their days there.

The green school movement has gained popularity as climate change and compounding research suggest that the overuse of natural resources and global warming are requiring a rethinking in how we live. As of 2019, approximately 9%–12% of schools in the United States have some type of green school program, and "more one third of all K–12 schools use outdoor gardens, natural classrooms and onsite habitats as part of their educational approach" (Coyle, 2020, p. 385). Eco-Schools, the largest global sustainable school program, has registered green schools in 77 countries, involving over 59,000 schools across the world (1994). Approximately 60% of K–12 schools in Hong Kong belong to a national Green School Network called Green Power, which focuses on developing environmentally focused curriculum, eco-monitoring, waste reduction and recycling. In the U.S., there are 300 sustainability coordinators that work in medium and large K–12 school districts (P. Beierle, personal communication, March 25, 2021), with a 15%–20% per year growth. To achieve a greater number of schools identifying as a "green school," an understanding of how to navigate terminology, finding appropriate resources and clarifying goals are needed.

The Emergence of Green Schools

Over the last 40–50 years, educational initiatives have sought to establish a new paradigm for PreK–12 schools that goes beyond the traditional classroom through projects that emphasize "learning beyond the classroom, reorienting school infrastructure" and engaging learners (Tilbury & Wortman, 2005, p. 22). One of those initiatives is the United Nations Sustainable Development Goals (SDGs), which have established a blueprint for how to "tackle climate change and work to preserve our oceans and forests" (UN, 2021, para. 1). The 17 SDGs, which were put into practice in January 2016 and were established as part of Agenda 2030 by the UN General Assembly, focus on the following:

Vienna International School, Vienna, Austria Promoting SDGs

Over the past four years, Vienna International School (VIS), integrated the UN Sustainable Development Goals (SDGs) into their curriculum. VIS has a certified ESD-School coordinator who is also a Global Schools Advocate that has embedded a sustainability strand in the science curriculum and promotes the social, economic and political aspects of the SDGs into all aspects of the schools community. Teachers are also trained in how to integrate EE concepts into all subject areas.

- ◆ Poverty eradication. Poverty reduction is inextricably linked to health and sustainable development.
- ◆ Sustainable consumption and production.
- ◆ Governance.
- ◆ Urban development.
- ◆ Environmental sustainability (UN, 2021).

Various organizations have taken the call from the UN to incorporate the SDGs into their own mission and vision. For example, Eco-Schools, which was established by the Foundation for Environmental Education (FEE), a non-governmental, non-profit organization, has eight Educational Principles that guide their work in environmental education and sustainability:

1. Ensure that participants are engaged in the learning/teaching process

2. Empower participants to take informed decisions and actions on real life sustainability issues
3. Encourage participants to work together actively and involve their communities in collaborative solutions
4. Support participants to examine their assumptions, knowledge, and experiences, in order to develop critical thinking, and to be open to change
5. Encourage participants to be aware of cultural practices as an integral part of sustainability issues
6. Encourage participants to share inspirational stories of their achievements, failures, and values, to learn from them, and to support each other
7. Continuously explore, test, and share innovative approaches, methodologies, and techniques
8. Ensure that continuous improvements through monitoring and evaluation are central to our programs (FEE, 2001, para. 1).

Eco-Schools also has a Seven Step process that requires schools to focus on "environmental, climate and sustainability issues," (FEE, 2001, para. 8). See Figure 1.1 and Chapter 3 for a more detailed approach to developing a green school.

After schools complete the Seven Step process, they can apply for the Green Flag Award, though that is usually after two years of program implementation. Schools can continue to achieve up to four Green Flags, at which point they are considered a permanent Eco-School. This achievement means that sustainability has been integrated into all aspects of the school's culture. Between 2011 and 2019, there were 141 U.S. schools that had achieved the highest honor of four green flags.

Another organization that connects to the UN SDGs and promotes sustainability in schools is the Global Environmental Education Partnership (GEEP). Established in 2014, the GEEP's mission is to "create a vibrant and inclusive learning network designed to build capacity in countries around the world to strengthen environmental education leading to a more

FORM AN
ECO-COMMITTEE

PRODUCE AN
ECO-CODE

CARRY OUT AN
ENVIRONMENTAL
REVIEW

INFORM &
INVOLVE

LINK TO THE
CURRICULUM

MONITOR &
EVALUATE

MAKE AN
ACTION PLAN

FIGURE 1.1 Eco-Schools seven-step process

CREDIT Eco-Schools, Foundation for Environmental Education (FEE) www.fee.global

sustainable future" (para. 1). Using environmental education and citizen engagement as the foundation, the GEEP organization strives to focus on the following:

◆ Professional development
◆ Globalization of environmental education standards guidelines
◆ Legislation and national-level policies that support environmental education
◆ Access to effective and promising practices
◆ Research and evaluation
◆ How environmental education can best address key issues, such as climate change, water shortages, and loss of biodiversity (2021)

Taiwan, one of the original partners of the GEEP organization, established the Taiwan EE Act (TEEA) in 2011 (TEEA, 2011). The TEEA goal is "for people to understand their ethical relationship with the environment, as well as to improve environmental knowledge, skills, attitudes, and values" (GEEP, 2021, para. 2), and requires that, "all students and any staff in government and business engage in 4 hours of government funded environmental education curriculum each year" (GEEP, 2021, para. 1).

The U.S. has also provided leadership in developing and supporting green schools. In 2011, numerous non-profit organizations, including the Center for Green Schools, the National Wildlife Federation and the Campaign for Environmental Literacy, came together to request the U.S. Department of Education, "honor schools for their sustainable facilities, health practices, and effective environmental education" (2021, para. 1). The Green Ribbon School award (ED-GRS) was created from this petition, and through 2021, the U.S Department of Education has recognized 489 PreK–12 schools, 92 school districts (started in 2013) and 54 postsecondary institutions (started in 2015). With 98,300 public schools and 34,576 private schools in the U.S., less than 1% of these schools have achieved the ED-GRS award (NCES, 2020), with approximately 20 states not submitting ED-GRS applications. The ED-GRS is a recognition award only; the schools do not receive any ED funding. Also, ED-GRS schools are not certified, though some U.S. states may connect the ED-GRS to existing state-based certification programs (2020). To further engage schools, Green Strides was created as the outreach arm of the ED-GRS award, with webinars, videos and resources that highlight a connection to the environment, sustainability, reducing environmental impact and health and wellness (2013).

Green schools are relatively new; their historical background dates back only a few decades. The establishment of the U.S. Green Building Council (USGBC) in 1993 and the launching of Eco-Schools in 1994 by the Foundation for Environmental Education (FEEE) in Europe were impactful in the development of green schools (Iwan & Rao, 2017). In 2000, the USGBC created the Center for Green Schools (CGS), and the FEEE became a global non-governmental organization (NGO) in 2001 and simplified its acronym to FEE.

> Importantly, major public school districts such as Atlanta, Austin, Baltimore, Fairfax County, Houston, Philadelphia, and New York City are using Eco Schools to encourage students to participate in implementing sustainability goals by conducting energy audits, tracking recycling performance, planting trees and gardens for climate mitigation and more. The fact that NWF Eco Schools U.S.A. is part of an international network of Eco Schools also helps connect these schools with green schools in other nations. (Coyle, 2020, p. 397)

As of 2019, Eco-Schools has nearly 20 million students participating in their programs in over 55,000 schools and 68 nations (National Wildlife Federation).

Connection to Environmental Education and Sustainability

The green school movement has been evolving for the last couple of decades, with the field of environmental education (EE) being considered a foundation to the movement. EE focuses on "how people and nature can exist in productive harmony" (NAAEE, n.d., para. 3). The U.S. Environmental Protection Agency (EPA), currently a leader in emphasizing EE, provides the following EE definition: "environmental education is a process that allows individuals to explore environmental issues, engage in problem solving, and take action to improve the environment. As a result, individuals develop a deeper understanding of environmental issues and have the skills to make informed and responsible decisions" (U.S. EPA, 2021, para. 1). The EPA also has a list of the components of what should be gained from EE.

♦ Awareness and sensitivity to the environment and environmental challenges.

- ◆ Knowledge and understanding of the environment and environmental challenges.
- ◆ Attitudes of concern for the environment and motivation to improve or maintain environmental quality.
- ◆ Skills to identify and help resolve environmental challenges.
- ◆ Participation in activities that lead to the resolution of environmental challenges (U.S. EPA, 2021, para. 2).

Environmental education (EE) has a plethora of connections to important educators and movements over the last two hundred years – specifically, Jean-Jacques Rousseau, who favored a careful stewardship of nature, and Anna Botsford Comstock, who in 1895 began a nature study program that took teachers and students outdoors to study the environment. The 1970s, as a decade, was instrumental in establishing important EE policy and organizations to support it. As part of the foundational aspects of EE, in 1970, the first Earth Day was started, which was also the same year as the first National Environmental Education Act (U.S. EPA, 2021) and the establishment of the National Association for Enviromental Education (now the North American Association for Environmental Education, or NAAEE). Just five years later, the Belgrade Charter, written by the United Nations Education, Scientific, and Cultural Organization and the 1977 Intergovernmental Conference on Environmental Education in Tibilisi were also impactful events that helped to establish EE.

The last thirty years have included the National Environmental Education Act (NEEA) of 1990 authorizing an EE office at the federal level, the UN General Assembly passing a resolution declaring 2005–2014 as the Decade of Education for Sustainable Development and, in 2013, the seventh World Environmental Education Congress focusing on the role of EE to empower outcomes, establish EE partnerships and mainstream EE and sustainability (NEEA, 1990). The NEEA of 1990 and the world conferences allow us to better understand the progress and ongoing gaps associated with environmental education.

Unlike EE, the term "sustainable development" has been around just since the 1970s and was introduced as a solution to growth problems and the ecological crisis. Sustainable development refers to a "condition of ecological and economic stability that is sustainable far into the future" (Meadows, 1972, p. 24). Formally, sustainability was featured in the 1972 declaration of the United Nations Conference on the Human Environment, which highlighted that "development needed to be sustainable – it should not focus only on economic and social matters, but also on matters related to the use of natural resources" (Du Pisani, 2006, p. 92). In 1987, the Brundtland Commission submitted a report, entitled *Our Common Future*, which emphasized the need for the application of "integrated, sustainable solutions to a broad range of problems related to population, agriculture and food security, biodiversity, energy choices, industry, and more" (Du Pisani, 2006, p. 92).

The need for sustainable development comes from humanity's demand on the planet, called "the ecological footprint," which explains that the Earth has a finite amount of biologically pro-ductive areas (Lin, 2018). For example, we need to grow plants for food and timber for shelter as well as standing forests that can absorb carbon dioxide emissions emanating from the use of fossil fuels, though with an increasing human population, we are using more of the Earth's resources than can regenerate in any given year. Scientists have been measuring the world's eco-logical footprint since the early 1990s, and as of 2014, we would need 1.7 planet Earths to maintain our global biocapacity (Global Footprint Network, 2021).

With humans going beyond the capacity of the Earth to regenerate, beginning in the 1970s, the development of renew-able sources of energy – such as wind turbines, solar panels, geothermal, biomass and hydropower – along with recycling and reusing became more prevalent (U.S. Energy Information Administration, 2020). As of 2020, 28% of global electricity came from the use of renewables (International Energy Agency). With the cost of solar panels decreasing and the advances in electric cars to be able to go longer distances, many countries are rethinking the use of fossil fuels. The hope is that practical

CREDIT Phoebe Beierle

solutions, such as renewable sources of energy, will help to provide solutions to today's sustainability problems. Grant High
School in Portland, Oregon, was renovated in 2019 and included
high-efficiency natural-gas-fired boilers/heaters that supply
hot water to low-flow plumbing fixtures and baseboard heaters
throughout the school (Photo 1.1). Energy use at Grant High
School is monitored by a building automation system that can
be fine-tuned for maximum efficiency, with the school achieving
LEED Gold certification.

Green Schools and the Organizations That Influence and Support Them

There is a fair amount of overlap among the programs
that support the greening of schools with the U.S.
Green Building Councils LEED program, NWF Eco
Schools U.S.A., Project learning Tree Green Schools, The

Green Schools Alliance, state green school programs in Kansas, Maryland, Oregon, Pennsylvania, Wisconsin, and numerous other states, with the total count of official green school programs roughly between 12,000 and 15,000 Pre-K–12 schools. (Coyle, 2020, p. 398)

Many of these organizations have similar goals, though some are more active and nationally or internationally focused. The Collaborative for High Performance Schools (CHPS) focuses on creating quality K–12 facilities that conserve resources, "maximize the health, well-being, and performance of students, educators and staff" and "practice good stewardship within schools to achieve community environmental and social goals" (2019, para. 5). Eco-Schools has high quality resources, such as energy and biodiversity audits broken down by grade level (K–2, 3–5, 6–8 and 9–12). The Green Schools Alliance focuses on energy savings and increasing school purchasing power. Though this is not an exhaustive list of organizations, it provides a good overview of what green school organizations can do to support PreK–12 schools.

Eco-Schools
As discussed in the first section, Eco-Schools, through the FEE, has been an early influencer of green schools. For more than a decade, the National Wildlife Federation (NWF) has been the U.S. host for Eco-Schools and currently has 5,000 K–12 schools registered (2021). Schools can gain a bronze or silver award through a self-assessment, though to achieve the Green Flag Award, an assessment by a program administrator is required. In Photo 1.2, Vienna International School in Vienna, Austria, has an Eco Board, where information is shared with their school community. It is changed often to keep the school community informed of local projects, as well as the school's participation in world campaigns.

Center for Green Schools
The Center for Green Schools (CGS) was launched in 2013 and has 27 member organizations in 26 participating countries.

CREDIT Marti Hendrichs, Vienna International School

The CGS shares resources, collaborates and networks across organizations. The School Sustainability Leader's Network (SSLN) was developed by the CGS to work with 300 U.S. K–12 school districts, specifically medium to large districts to support sustainability efforts. Their mission is "to inspire, train and support sustainability champions in an approach that integrates vision, systems thinking, reflection and climate solutions" (Center for Green Schools, 2020, para. 2).

Green Schools Alliance

Since 2007, the Green Schools Alliance (GSA) has connected over 13,000 schools from 49 U.S. states and 91 countries (2021). The main focus is reducing the carbon footprint of participating schools. One such program uses the collective power of the schools to purchase products and services to save money as well as buy items that are sustainable or environmentally friendly. Therre is also an energy tracking system, student-led challenges and curricula that teachers can access.

Green Schools Initiative

Founded in 2004, the Green Schools Initiative (GSI) was developed by parents interested in the "environmental health and ecological sustainability" of their children's schools (2005). The concerned parents focus on incorporating stewardship into teaching, supporting sustainable use of resources, and eliminating the use of toxins in schools. Their goals are to train educators (2,000 teachers from 350 schools have been trained so far), provide tools and resources and advocate for environmental policy change.

Green Schools National Network

The Green Schools National Network (GSNN) publishes the only digital magazine that focuses on sustainability, green school innovations and the health and well-being of school communities (2008). The Green Schools Catalyst Quarterly (GSCQ) features articles that include practical strategies, case studies and research (2021). The GSNN was created in 2008 by teachers, principals and superintendents and emphasizes core values such as transforming the educational system through increasing student voices, "high-quality professional learning opportunities for teachers" and developing innovation "through collaboration with sustainability change makers" (GSNN, para. 4). Partnering with Auburn University, GSNN has created a ten-module online course that helps PreK–12 leaders "explore curriculum, facility management, and leading change for whole school sustainability" (GSNN, 2008, para. 2).

International School Grounds Alliance and Green Schoolyards America

Both the International School Grounds Alliance (ISGA) and Green Schoolyards America (GSA) work in collaboration to "transform asphalt-covered school grounds into park-like green spaces that improve children's well-being, learning, and play while contributing to the ecological health and resilience of our cities" (GSA, 2013, para. 1). These organizations work closely with schools to replace asphalt and paved surfaces with interactive, innovative spaces that weave learning with the landscape, enhance the local environment and provide an aesthetically pleasing place for students and teachers. The organizations provide professional development, resources and case studies that can help schools make their own landscape changes.

Green Strides

Green Strides is a resource website of the U.S. Department of Education, in collaboration with the Center for Green Schools. It is intended to support schools who want information about the ED-GRS application process as well as provides an opportunity to learn about projects other schools are completing. For example, there is a sample school sustainability policy, green building standards and a clean energy resolution that can be used as models for schools interested in developing their own.

Institute for the Built Environment

The mission of the Institute for the Built Environment, established at Colorado State University, states, "We help you create healthy, thriving built environments through services that simplify and amplify your sustainability efforts" (IBE, 1994, para. 1). IBE is a non-profit organization that helps organizations, communities and teams create green buildings and successfully achieve a Leadership in Energy and Environmental Design (LEED) certification.

A project example focuses on the state of Missouri, which integrates the Whole School Sustainability Framework (Center for Green Schools, 2013) with the Missouri Environmental Education Association, Missouri Green Schools (MGS) project, the U.S. Department of Educations' Green Ribbon Schools (ED-GRS) and the Green Schools Alliance. Part of this initiative is to help Missouri schools achieve the Green Ribbon award. Parkway School District (PSD) in Chesterfield, Missouri, Mary Institute Country Day School in St. Louis, Missouri, and Sunrise School in Desoto, Missouri, were designated Green Ribbon Schools in January 2020.

National Green Schools Society

Though the National Green Schools Society (NGSS) has only been around since 2017, the organization is very student-focused and engages K–12 students who "achieve extraordinary impact in schools and communities" (NGSS, para. 4). The parent organization is Project Green Schools, which also focuses on recognizing change makers and supporting a national youth council. There is also a connection to science, technology, engineering and math (STEM), energy, public health and gaining college readiness skills. NGSS is not affiliated with the Next Generation of Science Standards, though they do support the implementation of STEM standards. The NGSS is active in 45 U.S. states, 45 countries and 6,500 schools and impacts over 500,000 students. NGSS supports an international Green Schools Society, National Youth Council and Green Difference Awards that are given out to students, teachers, principals and other school leaders who support outstanding environmental education and STEM efforts.

Conclusions

Almost 20% of the U.S. population spend their days in PreK–12 schools. Creating quality indoor and outdoor spaces and a healthy environment for learning should be a top priority for governments and organizations that support PreK–12 education. Though green schools are a relatively recent phenonemon, climate change and unsustainable use of natural resources are increasing their popularity. The foundation of green schools comes from both the environmental education (EE) and sustainable development movements. Numerous non-profit organizations have been created that focus on supporting sustainability practices in PreK–12 schools, including Eco-Schools, the Foundation for Environmental Education, Center for Green Schools and the Green Schools Alliance. These organizations help schools increase their purchasing power, offer quality sustainability curriculum and highlight the good work being accomplished in many PreK–12 green schools.

Questions to Consider

♦ What non-profit organizations might be able to support your sustainability work?

♦ Review the Eco-Schools Green Flag award (www.nwf.org/ Eco-Schools-U.S.A./Awards/Green-Flag). How might you begin the process to apply for the Bronze and Silver awards (which are self-assessed)?

♦ What resources does your state offer in relation to the Green Ribbon award (ED-GRS) or other state-sponsored environmental initiatives?

References

Center for Green Schools. (2020). *Global coalition for green schools*. www. centerforgreenschools.org/

Collaborative for High Performance Schools. (2019). *What we do*. https:// chps.net/what-we-do

Coyle, K. J. (2020). Green schools in the United States. In A. Gough & N. Gough (Eds.), *Green schools globally, international explorations in Outdoor and environmental education* (pp. 385–401). Springer Publishing.

Du Pisani, J. A. (2006). Sustainability development: Historical roots of the concept. *Environmental Sciences*, *3*(2), 83–96.

Foundation for Environmental Education (FEE). (2001). *Educational principles*. www.ecoschools.global/educational-principles

Global Environmental Education Partnership (GEEP). (2021). *Environmental education around the world*. https://thegeep.org/

Global Footprint Network. (2021). *How many earths?* www.footprint network.org/

Green School Alliance (GSA). (2021). *Programs for sustainable champions*. www.greenschoolsalliance.org/program

Green School Catalyst Quarterly. (2021). *K-12 Online green school magazine*. https://catalyst.greenschoolsnationalnetwork.org/gscatalyst/ Store.action

Green Schools Initiative (GSI). (2005). *Teach green*. www.greenschools. net/article.php-list=type&type=26.html

Green Schools National Network (GSNN). (2021). *Green school's catalyst quarterly*. https://greenschoolsnationalnetwork.org/gscq/

Green Schoolyards America. (2013). *Green schoolyard transformations*. www.greenschoolyards.org/

Green Strides. (2013). *Tools to green your school*. www.greenstrides.org/

IBISWorld. (2020). *Public schools in the U.S.: Employment statistics 2001–2026*. www.ibisworld.com/industry-statistics/employment/public-schools-united-states/

Institute for the Built Environment. (1994). *Institute for the built environment*. https://ibe.colostate.edu/

Iwan, A., & Rao, N. (2017). The green school concept: Perspectives of stakeholders from award-winning green preschools in Bali, Berkeley, and Hong Kong. *Journal of Sustainability Education*, *16*, 1–23.

Lin, D., Hanscom, L., Murthy, A., Galli, A., Evans, M., Neill, E., Mancini, M. S., Martindill, J., Medouar, F. Z., Huang, S., & Wackernagel, M., (2018). Ecological footprint accounting for countries: Updates and results of the national footprint accounts, 2012–2018. *Resources*, *7*(3), 58–80.

Meadows, D. H. (1972). *The limits to growth: A report of the club of Rome's project on the predicament of mankind*. Universe Books.

National Center for Education Statistics (NCES). (2020). *Back to school statistics*. https://nces.ed.gov/fastfacts/display.asp?id=372#PK12_teachers

National Wildlife Federation (NWF). (2021). *Eco schools U.S.A*. www.nwf.org/Eco-Schools-USA.aspx.

North American Association for Environmental Education. (n.d.). *About EE and why it matters*. https://naaee.org/

School Sustainability Leader's Network. (2020). *Vision and mission*. www.sustainabilityleadersnetwork.org/about-us/

Taiwan Environmental Education Act. (2011). *The environmental education act*. https://thegeep.org/learn/countries/taiwan

Tilbury, D., & Wortman, D. (2005). Whole school approaches to sustainability. *Geographical Education*, *18*, 22–30.

United Nations (UN). (2021). *Sustainable development goals*. https://sdgs.un.org/goals.

U.S. Department of Education. (2020). *Green ribbon schools*. https://www2.ed.gov/programs/green-ribbon-schools/index.html.

U. S. Department of Education, Office of Communications and Outreach. (2021). *Green ribbon schools: Highlights from the 2021 honorees.* https://www2.ed.gov/programs/green-ribbon-school/perform ance.html.

U. S. Energy Information Administration. (2020). *Renewable energy explained.* www.eia.gov/energyexplained/renewable-sources/

U.S. EPA. (1990). *National environmental education act.* www.epa.gov/ education/national-environmental-education-act

U.S. EPA. (2021). *Environmental education.* www.epa.gov/education/ what-environmental-education

2

Whole School Framework and the Green Ribbon Award

"The greatest threat to our planet is the belief that someone else will save it."

Robert Swan (2002)

Vignette

Mrs. Benken had been the principal at Taft Elementary for five years and was ready to begin the new school year. She had been interested in revising the school vision statement to better reflect the environmental initiatives they had been implementing for the last couple of years. The Green Team had created new communication pathways between grades and disciplines, which produced synergy among the teachers and school staff. The outdoor classroom was being used often, and the compost program being run by the Green Team in conjunction with the cafeteria staff had really taken off, with some teachers implementing it as part of their curriculum. Mrs. Benken felt that it was time to define clear goals that provided the school and community a sense of purpose and reflected the school's investment in

DOI: 10.4324/9781003164524-2

sustainability practices. She was excited to discuss her ideas at the first faculty meeting.

Chapter Objectives

◆ Highlight the Department of Education's Green Ribbon Award and the three pillars of sustainability.

◆ Explain the *Whole School Sustainability Framework* (WSSF) and how it can be applied to PreK–12 education.

◆ Provide typical characteristics of sustainable schools and how interconnectedness can be achieved among projects, curricula and communities.

The Green Ribbon Award and the Three Pillars of Sustainability

Picture your typical classroom with four walls, a chalkboard covering much of the wall space, 25–30 desks with attached chairs and a teacher's area squashed somewhere in the back of the room. Is this a space that you would look forward to spending nine to ten hours a day (Photo 2.1)?

Now, consider a green classroom where students congregate around moveable tables, plants are interspaced around the room and the walls are painted a soothing color with pictures interspersed for aesthetics. There are also opportunities for individual, small-group or large-group learning. In Photo 2.2, students at the Instructional Technology room at Colegio Santa Francisca Romana are sitting in lime-green chairs looking at computer screens. There are three wooden columns interspersed around the room that look like trees. There is a large window that lets in natural light.

Across the U.S.A. and around the world, schools and school districts are making a commitment to creating quality learning spaces that take the environment, aesthetics and sustainability into consideration. With the creation of the Green Ribbon

CREDIT iStock

CREDIT Kattia Marcela Lozada Mariño, Colegio Santa Francisca Romana

Schools (ED-GRS), the Center for Green Schools (CGS) began in earnest. Created in 2010, the mission of the CGS is to green every PreK–12 school in the U.S. In 2018, there were 130,930 public and private schools in the United States, with approximately a third of them having some type of green building policy (CGS, 2018).

The ED-GRS is a small but important part of the "greening movement," with research showing schools that received the ED-GRS had improved the quality of teaching and learning and community engagement and increased student engagement, such as student attention, curiosity and interest (Sterrett et al., 2014). The goal of this program is to "inspire schools, districts and Institutions of Higher Education (IHEs) to strive for 21st century excellence by highlighting promising practices and resources that all can employ. To that end, the award recognizes schools, districts, and IHEs that:

1. Reduce environmental impact and costs;
2. Improve the health and wellness of schools, students, and staff; and
3. Provide effective environmental and sustainability education" (ED-GRS, 2020, para 1).

Each year, schools, districts and postsecondary institutions are nominated based on the previous three pillars. Each year, states are allowed to nominate up to five PreK–12 schools or school districts and one postsecondary institution.

Using the *Whole School Sustainability Framework* (WSSF) as a Roadmap to Create a Sustainable School

The Institute for the Built Environment, out of Colorado in the U.S., in conjunction with the Center for Green Schools, developed the Whole School Sustainability Framework in 2014 (see Figure 2.1), which emphasizes an approach for "successful whole-school sustainability efforts" (Barr et al., 2014, p. 3). The goal behind the framework is to provide an opportunity for students to be educated in healthy environments where schools optimize natural light, support outdoor experiences and improve health, safety and efficiency. The framework is not considered a rating scale but more of a guide that provides a

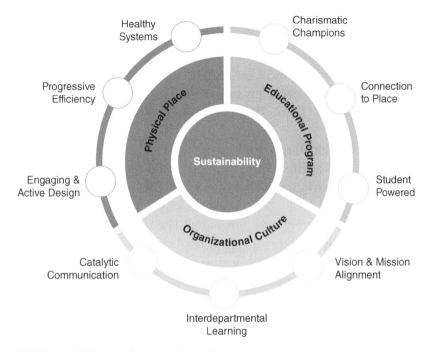

FIGURE 2.1 WSSF, Center for Green Schools (2014)

CREDIT Center for Green Schools and the Institute for the Built Environment at Colorado State University

path towards sustainability. In the following sections, each area of the framework will be discussed with examples of how it can be implemented.

As part of research by Plevyak et al. (2019), additional themes beyond the WSSF were created. Those themes, incorporated with the WSSF, will be highlighted in the next section and explain what is needed to create a successful green school. There is no order of importance as to how the themes are arranged.

- ◆ School Culture
- ◆ Curriculum Integration (connectedness between curriculum and sustainability projects)
- ◆ Common Student Experiences (recycling, gardening, water quality, energy, student clubs)
- ◆ Longevity (leadership, community)
- ◆ Student Voice (empowered by teachers)

- Personal Passion of People Involved and Administrative Oversight (to help guide the process)
- Supportive Community/Partnerships with Non-profits, Universities and Companies
- Location (school grounds)
- Finances (grants, budgetary item)

Vision and Mission Alignment

How do you excite your students, other teachers, staff and school administrators so that they WANT to include an environmental focus as part of your school's mission? The first step is to consider the school culture and review school groups and committees to see if any would be aligned with environmental practices. Think about specific people that you know who have a passion for recycling, engage with Earth Day projects or seem willing to support this endeavor. To get a true sense of interest, a short survey given out to a random sample of the student body, teachers, staff and administrators might make sense.

> **Eatonville Elementary Eatonville, Washington Transformation Time!**
>
> A complete "redo" occurred at Eatonville Elementary with environmental concepts integrated into the school's literacy, math and STEM program and a focus on a hands-on learning format. The school has also partnered with a nonprofit organization to develop a three-acre farm with a goal for providing sustainable crops. There are also national park service staff that support and help guide the sustainability projects.

Once you get an idea of how the school community will respond to this initiative, consider what goals you want to establish. Do you want to take small steps and develop an after-school program where a small number of students are engaged, or do you want to overhaul the school's curriculum and have essentially all students engaged with environmental initiatives?

Monroe Elementary (Hinsdale, Illinois) created sustainability committees that support self-esteem and life skills through environmental projects and gardening. Three years later, Monroe Elementary won the U.S. Blue Ribbon award for academics after revitalizing their living classroom.

Interdepartmental Learning

Ultimately, the goal of WSSF is to take a "systems-based approach" that permeates all disciplines and grade levels (Barr et al., 2014, p. 6) and has a high connectedness between curriculum and sustainability projects. At Monroe Elementary, they take a transdisciplinary approach (see Figure 2.2) to learning by integrating problem-based learning with sustainability. This approach breaks down the content silos and organizes learning through the use of real-world problems. For example, the milkweed was slowly disappearing from the Monroe Elementary garden, and they had the students conduct research on the cause and develop solutions as to how to successfully grow it the next season.

Along with making changes to the curriculum, a sea change in the way we teach may be required. Consider how the majority of teaching is conducted across the globe mainly through auditory learning with an emphasis on teacher lecture (Rutkienė & Tandzegolskiene, 2015). It is rare to see active application and promotion of critical thinking as the dominant mode of learning. Some visuals, such as a presentation, may be used, but they are focused on abstract learning. Other than kindergarten through third grade, much of the content is also taught through the siloed approach, where each area (science, social studies, math

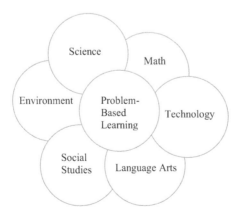

FIGURE 2.2 Transdisciplinary approach to learning

CREDIT Linda H. Plevyak, PhD

and language arts) is taught separately from each other. So considering a change to an integrated, problem-based learning approach may require additional effort, though in terms of student achievement, it will prove to be invaluable.

Catalytic Communication

As part of the change process, it is imperative that teachers communicate their ideas both inside the school and outside to parents, partners and community organizations. There are a number of ways that teachers (and potentially a specific Green Team committee) can share their ideas and projects with others, including the following:

- ◆ Present at a school board meeting.
- ◆ Have a grade-level/school fair or parent night.
- ◆ Create a friendly competition with another school, and share the results with the school district.
- ◆ Develop a website that highlights environmental projects, cost savings, etc.

Monroe Elementary Hinsdale, Illinois Dynamic Duo!

Over twenty years ago, two teachers decided that students needed to better understand their role in protecting the Earth. They created the Living Classroom Learning Lab, which includes a prairie, a butterfly garden, a Japanese garden, a vegetable garden, a pond and a bee habitat. The focus is on the interdependence of humans and nature. Both teachers have since retired, though they still actively engage with organizing volunteers and support the gardens.

Charismatic Champions

With anything that takes organization, persistence and connecting with others, having passionate people who care about sustainability are required to oversee and organize sustainability projects. If this person(s) is not in a leadership role, success will more likely be had if at least one school leader (principal or department head) is supportive. In the Fayette County Public Schools in Lexington, Kentucky, there is an energy and sustainability coordinator that helps schools monitor energy usage and supports individual school sustainability projects.

The ideal situation is to have a team that divides responsibilities and focuses on the strengths of each individual. For instance, if someone is a good writer, he/she might help with grant development. The goal would be that if someone integral to the team were to leave, the sustainability momentum would continue as there is an established culture in the building. Also, having an administrator on the team allows for quick decisions and is integral to the success of sustaining initiatives. Similarly, having a staff member engaged would be helpful as he/she can share ideas on practical items, such as how recycling materials will be sorted or picked up or how compost items will be buried in the garden or outdoor area.

Engaging and Active Design

The location of a school and its physical structure can provide an amazing opportunity for experiments, outdoor projects and analysis of nature. Being located by a mountain range, pond, lake, forest, farm or river can expand a school's physical space. For example, near the base of Mt. Rainier sits Eatonville Elementary, which has national park service staff that work closely with teachers on developing curricula, though some schools may not have accessible natural settings, so they may need to be developed through other means. For example, Legacy Elementary in Madison, Alabama, increased the height of their football field and, in so doing, created an ideal location for a pond and outdoor garden.

The school building itself can be a teaching tool that helps students understand how systems function. Consider having the students develop problem-based questions that focus on the school systems, such as heating, ventilation, energy and water usage. They could, with teacher oversight, collect and analyze data on these systems. For example, questions in relation to lighting could include "How efficient is the lighting in classrooms, the gym, the library and the cafeteria?" or "Does the lighting create a conducive environment for learning?" Research shows that in classrooms where natural light is used, students perform at about a 25% higher rate than when artificial lighting is utilized (NRC, 2007). More information about how to use school systems in your teaching will be discussed in Chapter 6.

Progressive Efficiency

Clear goals and communicating progress towards these goals both internally and externally will energize and guide the school community. The more that progress and results are shared, the more likely it is that the local community (neighbors, local organizations, businesses) will be interested in becoming involved. To engage others, teachers could include a story about students or that a particular project had an impact. At Gove Elementary in Belle Glade, Florida, the University of Florida helped teachers and students create a barn owl house. The elementary school also has a strong connection with the two high schools in their district, with the high school students volunteering their time to support sustainability projects. These outside entities were personally invited to join in supporting projects taking place at the school. Having more of these types of connections means that processes get institutionalized and will continue into the future, even if a key person leaves the school.

Healthy Systems

What do you envision when you think about the health of your school? Maybe you think of air quality, the food that is served, or how people interact with each other? The school itself is an ecosystem, where each part depends on the other to survive and grow. For example, school leaders set the tone for others to follow in relation to behavior and communication. The sustainability system is similar in that teachers, students, staff and administrators work together to create a healthy environment, which may include getting food from locally sourced farms that emphasize organic practices. In turn, a compost system within the school that ties back to the same farms will limit waste. This interconnectedness strengthens the overall health and well-being of the people who eat meals in the school.

Connection to Place

The use of the outdoors can promote student learning as well as develop an appreciation for nature. Examples of what can be developed on school grounds include creating a butterfly, hummingbird or edible garden, building paths through the woods, developing a living classroom learning lab, using a beehive as an observation area or planting native fauna to repair erosion along a riverbank. This type of integration of the outdoors with the learning process wouldn't happen without volunteers and support from the community. Meadowthorpe Elementary works with the University of Kentucky to renovate the garden area next to the school to avoid the use of lawnmowers.

Using parent expertise, Monroe Elementary had volunteers plan the vegetable and Japanese gardens, prairie, pond and observational beehive areas. The school also donates vegetables and fruits from the garden to a food pantry. At Legacy Elementary, Lowe's and Home Depot donated plants for the outdoor area, and the Alabama Outdoor Wildlife Federation donated fish for the pond. Parents, high school students and Boy Scouts help with weeding and gardening. Carnation Elementary works with local Native American tribes in planting trees and restoring the riparian zone on local rivers, with parents supporting the initiatives.

Student Powered

Student voice (empowered by teachers, staff, volunteers or community members) can be a powerful way to engage students in sustainability projects. They can help to establish groups, make decisions and create their own environmental projects, with younger students needing some monitoring by an adult. In creating a Green Team, a Meadowthorpe Elementary teacher has students monitor classrooms for energy usage and conduct an environmental audit (World Wildlife Federation audit, 2021). At Legacy Elementary, fifth graders work with second graders and use the pond area to highlight environmental concepts (e.g., building birdhouses for local bird species and planting sunflowers, oregano, cilantro, okra and tomatoes). There is also a group of students at Legacy Elementary that have taken ownership of maintaining the pond and adjacent area, such as mulching and clearing beds. Empowering students to make a difference can manifest itself in various ways. For example, the lunchroom can create a large amount of waste if unchecked. At Carnation Elementary, the student club is focused on decreasing the metal utensils that are thrown away during lunch, and having engaged with the director of food services, they are currently considering compostable utensils. In Photo 2.3, students at North Park School for Innovation are highlighting the recycle, trash and compost containers in their school.

These types of interactions likely don't meet the threshold of curriculum integration. For example, students may participate in recycling, gardening or energy audits (https://www.nwf.org/Eco-Schools-USA/Pathways/Audit), but this activity is likely not integrated into their daily schedule or a required part of the curriculum. It is possible to embed these empowering experiences for all students, as eighth graders at Park Avenue Elementary (Warwick, New York) are required to take ten weeks

CREDIT Jeff Cacek, Stan Mraz, North Park School for Innovation

of environmental education, and at Meadowthorpe Elementary, students are taken camping for two days with no electronics. A focus on the whole child that includes the social/emotional aspects of learning and growing can be accomplished through participating in garden clubs, planting trees, helping in a greenhouse, or participating in a fund drive to purchase a solar panel (or other materials). Monroe Elementary students' problemsolve, such as finding out why the milkweed disappeared last year. Teachers and administrators believe that students need to experience sustainability so they internalize and begin incorporating the practices in their daily lives.

Longevity

Research shows that it isn't so much about how long a school emphasizes sustainability but how interconnected the projects are with each other, the curriculum and the overall vision of the school (Warner & Elser, 2015). Also, having teachers and staff over time in the same roles – such as a Green Team overseeing projects, submitting grants and focusing on the vision of the school – will help in sustaining success. Of course, having an administrator, such as a principal or sustainability/STEM coordinator, providing longterm leadership contributes as well. The superintendent for Park Avenue Elementary in New York conducts a teacher mentoring program every year, and sustainability practices are part of this orientation. At Park Avenue Elementary, there is a "fantastic (cohesive) team of people who support the green school effort and we have a great relationship with the teacher's union" (J. Yap, personal communication, October 31, 2018).

Finances

Having funds available to purchase materials, support programming, conduct marketing or provide groups with travel support (to present at local or national conferences) can make you feel like you are positively impacting sustainability projects – though a small budget can go a long way, especially if you use parents and community members as your "labor force." There are numerous small and large grants available to schools who are interested in spending the time to apply (see Chapter 7 and the resource list for further grant information). Some administrators may be resistant to making environmental changes. For example, North Park School for Innovation (Columbia Heights, Minnesota) had difficulty acquiring the budget for compostable garbage bags and recycling bins until it was able to quantify an overall cost savings and received grant supports from Anoka County.

If schools revamp their physical plant and there are funds that come from the energy savings, teachers, with administrative support, could purchase environmental items (e.g., recycling containers, energy-efficient soda machines, rain barrels). Having multiple funding avenues is helpful to maintain forward momentum. Monroe Elementary received funds from a car company to build a green power car, holds fundraisers to support their garden, received funding through the PTO and also has a budget allocated from school funds. As part of a student club, Carnation Elementary had students help write a grant for water bottle stations. Gove Elementary received wellness grants, which they believe tie in nicely with the environment (which also includes a social/emotional focus).

Creating a Green School and How Interconnectedness Can Be Achieved

How do you view your work world? Do you enjoy your daily commute to work, find pleasure in your work space, have valuable interactions with others and feel your work adds positively to the local community and beyond? Your "universe" or your connections to the environment, physical structures and community are integral to your emotional, physical and spiritual health. For example, if you are stuck in traffic before your workday begins, it will likely affect your mood at least during some part of the day.

Photo 2.4 reflects how "aesthetics of space" can impact how you feel. For example, spending time in a beautiful space that has natural light, pleasing colors, plants and a symmetrical design will likely support a positive mood. This aesthetically pleasing space interconnects with the other aspects of

CREDIT Kattia Marcela Lozada Mariño, Colegio Santa Francisca Romana

your daily experiences, such as the people you meet, the work that you do, etc. (photo from Colegio Stanta Francisca Romana).

Creating a green school can be the catalyst for making major changes to the school structure, from the physical building to the curriculum. With planning and reflection, the school community (teachers, students, staff and administrators) can decide what components or characteristics are important to them. Birney and Reed (2009) created seven characteristics that support the development of an interconnected green school:

The same type of interconnectedness happens within a school. The environment (aesthetics of space), physical structure (walls, windows, natural vs. artificial light), teaching (curriculum and pedagogy) and community (emotional, physical or spiritual interactions with others) impact how teachers, staff and students feel about their world. Whether the people within a school go home at the end of the day feeling drained or energized says a lot about the interconnectedness of the school itself.

◆ Sustainable schools give attention to their broader social and ecological footprint;

- ◆ Sustainable schools view their ethos and purpose within a broader global context, and develop an understanding among stakeholders, including students, of that purpose;
- ◆ Sustainable schools create positive benefits for pupils including student engagement, participation, and leadership;
- ◆ Sustainable schools allow development, integration, and connection with other educational policies and initiatives;
- ◆ Sustainable schools provide direction and focus that bring about school improvements, including Every Child Matters (ECM) outcomes and supports raising achievement and attainment;
- ◆ Sustainable schools focus specifically on improving the learning of children; and
- ◆ Sustainable schools engage in curriculum change and development as sustainability is embedded across the whole curriculum (pgs. 24–32).

These types of changes can not only increase the quality of interactions and the way that you feel but can also provide a platform for higher quality and deeper learning experiences for students (Kariippanon et al., 2018; Kuo et al., 2018).

Conclusions

The Green Ribbon Award, through the U.S. Department of Education, is an important part of the "greening movement," which promotes sustainability within the curriculum, healthy living and a reduction of the environmental impact of the school facilities, grounds and operations. The Whole School Sustainability Framework can be used by schools as a roadmap to develop their own green school initiatives. Some of the important themes where schools can incorporate sustainability practices is in the school culture, curriculum and school grounds. Students should also have a voice in these sustainability initiatives. To begin the green school development process, there needs to be at least one person who is interested in sustainability practices. That person then builds a Green Team, which should include an administrator, staff and community members. Interconnecting a school's sustainability initiatives with the overall curriculum, health and wellness of teachers and students and school vision can be deeply impactful on students learning and understanding of the world.

Questions to Consider

♦ Review the Green Ribbon Award application online (https://www2.ed.gov/programs/green-ribbon-schools/index.html) and make note of the criteria. Are you able to apply? If not, what can you do to make application achievable in the next three to five years?
♦ Review the Whole School Framework. What aspects do you think your school does well, and what aspects do you need to improve upon?
♦ How could you interconnect sustainability to your school's vision, curriculum and school grounds? Consider taking on one of these aspects this school year.

References

Barr, S. K., Cross, J. E., & Dunbar, B. H. (2014). *The whole-school sustainability framework: Guiding principles for integrating sustainability into all aspects of a school organization*. https://www.usgbc.org/education/sessions/whole-school-sustainability-framework-10353101.

Birney, A., & Reed, J. (2009). *Sustainability and renewal: Finds from the learning sustainable schools research project*. National College for Leadership of Schools and Children's Services.

Kariippanon, K., Cliff, D., Lancaster, S., Okely, A., & Parrish, A. M. (2018). Perceived interplay between flexible learning spaces and teaching, learning and student wellbeing. *Learning Environments Research, 21*, 301–320. https://link.springer.com/article/10.1007%2Fs10984-017-9254-9.

Kuo, M., Browning, M., & Penner, M. (2018). Do lessons in nature boost subsequent classroom engagement? Refueling students in flight. *Frontiers in Psychology.* https://link.gale.com/apps/doc/A521387519/EAIM?u=ucinc_main&sid=EAIM&xid=a7470b09.

National Research Council. (2007). *Green schools: Attributes for health and learning.* https://www.nap.edu/read/11756/chapter/7#85.

Plevyak, L., Tamsukhin, S., & Gibson, R. (2019). Building a foundation for sustainable principles: Case studies of K–6 green ribbon schools. *Journal of Sustainability Education, 21,* 1–19.

Rutkienė, A., & Tandzegolskiene, I. (2015). Students' attitude towards learning methods for self-sufficiency development in higher education. *Proceedings of the International Scientific Conference, 1,* 291.

Sterrett, W. L., Imig, S., & Moore, D. (2014). U.S. department of education green ribbon schools: Leadership insights and implications. *Journal of Organizational Learning and Leadership, 12*(2), 1–18.

Swan, R. (2002). www.2041foundation.org.

U.S. Department of Education. (2020). *Green ribbon schools.* https://www2.ed.gov/programs/green-ribbon-schools/index.html.

U.S. Green Building Council. (2018). *Advancing green schools.* http://centerforgreenschools.org/.

Warner, B. P., & Elser, M. (2015). How do sustainable schools integrate sustainability education? *Journal of Environmental Education, 46*(1), 1–22.

World Wildlife Federation. (2021). *Environmental audits for K–2, 3–5, 6–8, and 9–12.* https://www.nwf.org/Eco-Schools-USA/Pathways/Audit.

3

Getting Started in Creating a Green School

"There is no such thing as 'away.' When we throw anything away it has to go somewhere."

Unknown

Vignette

Mr. Stein, the plant manager at Oak Middle School, had just finished talking with Mrs. Sena, who taught seventh grade. She was interested in the large concrete area in the back of the school that had little purpose now that the playground had been moved to the side of the building. It was a large space, approximately 200' × 150' (61 meters × 46 meters), that Mrs. Sena wanted to turn into an outdoor learning space. She was planning on submitting a grant to Green Schoolyards America (https://www.greenschoolyards.org/grant-opportunities) to fund the project, though she planned to talk with the principal first. It sounded like an interesting project, and Mr. Stein was intrigued about the actual design and what materials they could use to create a shelter. He planned on

DOI: 10.4324/9781003164524-3

doing some online research for ideas and looked forward to the meeting with Mrs. Sena and the principal next week.

Chapter Objectives

- ◆ Explain how creating a green school can improve numerous aspects of PreK–12 education.
- ◆ Focus on practical ways PreK–12 schools can create a vibrant green school that embeds sustainable ideas and projects into their mission and curriculum.
- ◆ Discuss the development and use of green space.
- ◆ Highlight a step-by-step process that staff and teachers can follow to create a green school.

Green Schools and the Connection to Quality Education

It isn't a matter of making the argument for creating a green school; it is really a question of why aren't all PreK–12 schools following the steps to incorporate sustainability into their mission and curriculum. Research shows that schools that promote sustainability through hands-on experiential learning and a healthy environment are "enhancing student outcomes and success, safeguarding the health of students and staff, and saving scarce funds while also reducing a school's environmental impact" (Sterrett et al., 2014, p. 3). This chapter will discuss the process for how teachers, administrators, community members, parents and others can feel confident that they have the tools to develop a green school.

So we shouldn't need to state reasons for creating an aesthetically pleasing environment where children WANT to go to school because they are involved in exciting experiential coursework, though it is understandable that people might be hesitant to dive in. Not everyone has the requisite knowledge and understanding needed to successfully implement the greening of a school. It is also a commitment of time, effort and resources that, in the short term, could take away from other projects. Though, with long-term thinking and enthusiasm, this process could alter the way teaching and learning occurs in schools.

Benefits to Teaching and Learning

Consider what the benefits will be for students, teachers, staff, parents and community members once the greening of the school has been implemented. A report completed in 2018 states that implementing environmental education has

> led to a number of positive impacts, from improving academic performance, to enhancing critical thinking skills, to developing personal growth and life-building skills including confidence, autonomy, and leadership. In addition, a number of the studies showed that environmental education increased civic engagement and positive environmental behaviors. (Ardoin et al., 2018; NAAEE, 2018, para. 2)

Also, a study by McKey (2017) that focused on Green Ribbon schools showed that "strong relationships exist between ecological and democratic principles" (p. 15). Providing a democratic structure where school leaders model equality, social justice and fairness seems to be a foundation for incorporating sustainability into a school. In 2014, Sterrett, Imig and Moore surveyed recipients of the Green Ribbon Award (ED-GRS), and the perception by school leaders was that these schools had improved the quality of teaching and learning and community engagement and increased student engagement (student attention, curiosity and interest). Another significant aspect of this survey was that 50% of the 2012–2014 Green Ribbon honorees were from disadvantaged schools, where at least 40% of the students qualified for a free or reduced lunch (Sterrett et al., 2014). This statistic shows that being a "disadvantaged school" was not a barrier to implementing sustainable practices or achieving the ED-GRS award.

Education for Sustainable Development (ESD) has been launched to "empower students with sustainability competencies through a holistic interdisciplinary perspective" that emphasizes "learner-centered democratic teaching strategies" (Boeve-de Pauw et al., 2015, p. 15694; Olsson et al., 2015). In a study with Swedish students in grades 6, 9, and 12, who were completing an ESD certificate, results showed that ESD "as a teaching approach induces sustainability consciousness among students" (Boeve-de Pauw et al., 2015, p. 15709). ESD also "stimulates students to ask questions, analyze, think critically and make good decisions" (Laurie et al., 2016, p. 231).

Consider asking students about how natural resources should be used: sustainably or through irreversible ecological change. A study that focused on comparing Eco-Schools with a control group of schools found that Eco-school students have "lower utilization values than control school students" (Boeve-de Pauw & Van Petegem, 2013, p. 96). Meaning, they wanted to see a more sustainable use of natural resources. In 1999, Maryland created the Green Schools Award Program (MDGS), and currently, there are 664 green schools, which is approximately 33% of the 2,200 public and independent schools in Maryland (Maryland Association for Environmental and Outdoor Education, 2021). A study of these schools showed there was "positive correlation between student achievement on math and English language arts standardized test scores and MDGS designation" (Ghent et al., 2014, p. 256).

In relation to pedagogical approaches, a study that focused on ESD-active schools surveyed teachers and showed that "as a designated group, they generally have a higher quality school improvement process and more coherent organizations with greater potential to support practical teaching and pedagogical work than ordinary schools," though the sample size was small (Mogren et al., 2019, p. 524). This study also showed that teachers in the ESD-active schools "recognized a holistic vision and its implementation in the evaluation, planning and execution of teaching" (Mogren et al., 2019, p. 525). Teachers that implement ESD use diverse methodologies with group discussions, interactive lectures, small-group research projects, interdisciplinary work, class debates, site visits and guided independent study as the most common (Borg et al., 2012). Teachers of different disciplines used the methods differently, with science and social science (except site visits) teachers using all of the methods and language teachers using group discussions (30%) and interdisciplinary work (27%) fairly frequently (Borg et al., 2012). This study also found that teachers have a positive attitude towards ESD, though they felt unprepared to teach it.

Ultimately, the study of the environment and sustainability practices go beyond scores on a test. Students are more motivated to learn when the topics and issues are connected to their own world and experiences in their community. Emphasizing problem-based skills and collaborative investigations go beyond content and comprehension skills and focus on application of ideas, analysis, and evaluation, which are difficult to include on a standardized test. When the focus of classrooms is on student-centered, hands-on inquiry with sustainability issues, students are taking away positive, sustained experiences that last a lifetime. In Photo 3.1, students from Colegio Los Nogales are experiencing the outdoors at the Macarena National Park in Meta, Colombia.

Legacy Elementary, Madison, Alabama, and Newport School, Bucaramanga, Colombia

Learning Through Experiences

At Legacy Elementary, the students experience the outdoors through the turtle habitat, pond, garden, outdoor classroom, fruit-tree planting and solar panels. There is also participation in environmental camp and growing vegetables (radishes, spinach), cotton, soybeans, potatoes and peanuts. Students also participate in workdays at the pond and science stations (with help from the high school students). There is a focus on healthy living at Newport School with an emphasis on being active citizens. Water, marine life and biodiversity are used as focal points as students learn about threatened bird species and understanding how to clean water in rural areas near their school.

Improvement to Human Health and Wellness

The 2021 State of Our Schools report highlights that the "PK–12 school facility infrastructure gap stood at $46 billion in 2016. In this year's study, we find that the school facilities annual funding gap has reached $85 billion a year, up $25 billion since 2016" (Filardo, 2021, p. 13). Providing a space that protects occupant

CREDIT Pedro Felipe Linares, Colegio Los Nogales

health and supports wellness is an important goal in creating a green school. Benefits of a healthy environment include improvement in employee and student productivity, efficient use of energy, water and other resources and a reduction of the overall impact on the environment (Kats, 2006). It can also save money as the most recent data show that the average functional age of school buildings is 19 years old ("functional age is based on the year of the most recent renovation or the year of construction if no renovation has occurred") (Bahr & Sparks, 2016, p. 4), and their inefficiencies can cost each school approximately $100,000 a year (Kats, 2006).

However, financial cost is not as important as the health and wellness of the people who spend 85%–90% of their day inside a school building where nearly one in 13 children has asthma (EPA, 2020). Childhood asthma is associated with over 10 million missed school days per year (Hus et al., 2016). As numerous research studies have shown, not only is classroom ventilation directly connected with student performance, (Haverinen-Shaughnessy et al., 2011; Hutter et al., 2013; Midouhas et al., 2018; Pulimeno et al., 2020), but filtration systems can also improve air quality and reduce asthma symptoms (Martenies & Batterman, 2018).

Teachers believe that, along with air quality, their teaching quality and student achievement is affected by the temperature in the room, and as such, being able to control the temperature in individual classrooms is "very important to student perform-ance" (Kats, 2006, p. 10). Lighting is another important factor to consider, with research showing that the use of natural and indirect lighting "improves test scores, reduces off-task behavior, and plays a significate role in the achievement of students" (Buckley et al., 2005, p. 1112). Providing "good indoor air quality, access to daylight and outside views and better acoustics" are important aspects for teachers as they consider where to teach and how long they stay (Rainwater & Hartke, 2011, p. 11).

School Location: Development and Use of Green Space

Research has shown that green space can facilitate health and well-being, promote physical activity and improve social interaction (World Health Organization, 2017). Creating a well-designed space on the school grounds can "model the ecologically-rich cities we would like to inhabit, at a smaller scale, and teach the next generation how to live more lightly on the Earth" (Danks, 2021, para. 2). The non-profit organization, Green Schoolyards America (https://www.greenschoolyards.org), works to "trans-form asphalt-covered school grounds into park-like green spaces that improve children's well-being, learning, and play while contributing to the ecological health and resilience of our cities" (Green Schoolyards America, 2021, para. 1). The photo sequence shows the evolution of a schoolyard transform-ation at Commodore Sloat Elementary School in San Francisco, California. The greening of this schoolyard occurred as a part of a citywide modernization bond that funded school updates as well as schoolyard greening throughout San Francisco Unified School District (Sharon Danks, Photos 3.2, 3.4, & 3.5 & Arden Bucklin-Sporer, Photo 3.3, 2005–2019).

CREDIT Sharon Danks, Green Schoolyards America

CREDIT Arden Bucklin-Sporer

CREDIT Sharon Danks, Green Schoolyards America

CREDIT Sharon Danks, Green Schoolyards America

Humans need green space to restore, refresh and destress. Increasingly, the global population, including approximately 50% of all children, live in an urban environment (UNICEF, 2021). It is estimated that in less than 30 years, "almost 70% of the world's children will live in urban areas, many of them in slums" (UNICEF, 2021, para. 1). Schools that provide a green space add to the natural beauty of the area and can improve the well-being of the school community (Akpinar, 2016). An ideal environmental location for a school might be near a pond, lake, river or ocean or in proximity to a mountain range, deciduous forest, grassland or desert. Being positioned near one of these locations may make it easier to have an environmentally focused school, though there are opportunities for schools in even the densest urban locations. Schools that have little to no green space can work with the facility manager and administration to consider what areas might not have much foot traffic and could be used for an outdoor classroom and/or green space development. This could also be a project that a student club could take on with teacher or administrative mentoring.

Step-by-Step Process of Greening a School

Beginning the process to create a green school essentially starts with the interest of one person, who can be called a "charismatic champion" (Barr et al., 2014, p. 13). This person can be anyone – a student, staff member, teacher or administrator and even people from the community. Having formal leaders, such as an administrator or a school board member, supporting the process is extremely helpful and can increase the rate of implementation.

This section will go into detail about the approach that the "charismatic champion" and team will take to get started with developing a green school. The individual items are not chronological as it is not important to follow them in a lockstep manner, though each point is important and should be included in the school's framework for achieving a green school. It is best to review each item and prioritize them in relation to your current situation.

◆ Have the Charismatic Champion(s) (CC) make a commitment to begin the green school process. One of the first tasks should be to talk with school leadership and the appropriate decision makers to make sure they are okay with a committee being developed. This permission should be in some type of written form (e.g., email or formal letter) in case there are leadership changes and you need to show legitimacy. It also helps with finding funding and enhancing the committee's credibility (Lieberman, 2013). Over time, once the program is established, gaining approval from the school board or even the state board of education can help with getting larger grants, changing school curriculum or requiring specific courses be taken by students.

> **Vermont School, Medellín, Colombia, and Odyssey Charter School, Wilmington, Delaware**
> **Urban Farming**
>
> Vermont School, near the second biggest city (Medellín) in Colombia, is 2,500 meters (8,202 feet) above sea level and surrounded by mountains, though students live in an urban environment. The school focuses on urban gardening and how to grow different plants in the students' apartments. With a student administered farmer's market, they are able to better understand the life cycle of plants. At Odyssey Charter School, located in a former DuPont office complex, they have 34 raised gardening beds, 18 chickens, two goats and two roosters. The students and the leader of the Green Team also hydroponically grow 3,000 pounds of vegetables each year, which is donated to the local community.

◆ It is helpful to have more than one person at the beginning, and it could be a topic that is brought up for discussion during a teacher-faculty meeting, the student orientation at the beginning of the year, a school board meeting or the development of a Green Team by administration. If a parent or community member is the CC, they will likely need internal support, though the Parent-Teacher Association (PTA) could also be a good place to start.

  • The CC should put together a set of ideas or plans *OR* enlist the help of others who are also interested in sustainability. One way to develop ideas is to interview "key stakeholders" such as custodians, principal, cafeteria staff or district personnel (Center for Green Schools, 2021, para. 3). If the CC is a student, it is likely they will need the support of an adult as they might not have the ability to put together a plan.

◆ Develop a team of interested participants (see the next section on team building) who are willing to help create an action plan. Once the Green Team has been established, the Center for Green Schools has a Getting Started Checklist that provides links to helpful resources (2021).

• Establish a mission statement that emphasizes the "core purpose of the program, its primary objectives, and how success will be measured" (Lieberman, 2013, p. 102). Next, consider what goals you want to accomplish. Is it important to raise academic achievement or increase student engagement? It could be that connecting content areas to sustainability takes precedence. Consider goals that support student learning and include students in the decision-making process. For example, if a short-term goal is to develop a garden or create a green space, have teams of students research ideas and develop design plans. An important note is that the overarching goal should be to have a healthy system "that balances environmental, social and economic concerns" (Barr et al., 2014, p. 11). For a successful school, another goal could be to create an environment where students, teachers and staff look forward to sharing experiences, focusing on physical, emotional and social health and achieving sustainability learning goals.

• Consider financial support opportunities. There are grants available that can provide funding for small projects ($250–$500 dollars), such as plants, mulch or signage. Large projects ($25,000–$50,000 dollars) could include solar panels or wind turbines. Some grant funding agencies want to see that the school has made a commitment to sustainability with either their own funding or infrastructure changes (such as upgrading the HVAC system or incorporating recycling/composting into daily activities). Financial support from the district office might occur once the Green Team has been established, has created goals and has shown that the team is actively looking for external funds. "Having multiple funding avenues is helpful to maintain forward momentum" (Plevyak et al., 2019, p. 12). Financial support will be discussed in more detail in Chapter 7.

- Discuss what materials and resources are required and who might be able to find these items either through an internal school request or by contacting a local business or organization. Establishing relationships with outside partners can help with gaining professional information, materials and support. Also, review standards and see if any match with sustainability concepts (see Chapter 5 for more information about connecting to standards). For example, search standards for "cycles, social justice, respect for limits, systems thinking, local and global citizenship, interconnectedness, the commons" (Barr et al., 2014, p. 14), sustainability, environmental science, biodiversity or ecology.

♦ Engage and communicate with other school members, including students, staff, administration, families and community members. Communicating through both formal (newsletter, meetings, handouts and bulletin boards) and informal (hallway chats, discussion during breaks or lunch and before and after meeting conversations) are part of the process of conveying information (Verhelst et al., 2020). Other ways to share about goals, the school vision and action items can be through an open house, school assemblies, school tours, student presentations, appreciation luncheon or invitation to join the Green Team.

◆ If you integrate ideas into the curriculum, it is a good idea to field-test ideas with interested teachers from one grade level. Consider incorporating ideas that focus on the local community and have a meaningful connection to students' lives. It will build a "sense of place" and promote a "high level of student engagement" (Lieberman, 2013, p. 125). Liberman states that field testing is an opportunity to assess instructional materials, including, "adequacy of background information, clarity of instructional procedures, utility of visual aids and reading materials, suitability for intended grade level, and efficacy of content, procedures, and assessments for targeted standards" (2013, p. 184).

- As science is a closely connected content area with sustainability, there are numerous Next Generation of Science Standards (NGSS) that align nicely, such as the following examples:
  - In kindergarten, there is a NGSS standard that highlights "interdependent relationships in ecosystems: animals, plants, and their environment" (2013, p. 6).
  - There is a middle school NGSS standard that emphasizes asking questions "to clarify evidence of the factors that have caused the rise in global temperatures over the past century" (2013, p. 59).
  - There is a high school NGSS standard that evaluates "the claims, evidence and reasoning that the complex interactions in ecosystems maintain relatively consistent numbers and types of organisms in stable conditions, but changing conditions may result in a new ecosystem" (2013, p. 83).
- Use thematic curriculum by integrating/embedding sustainable concepts into content areas (see Chapter 5 for more information about how to incorporate problem-solving and sustainability into the PreK–12 curriculum). Schools that have a high interconnectedness between curriculum and sustainability projects "view sustainability as a whole systems process that

permeates everything in and outside of the school" (Plevyak et al., 2019, p. 9). Assess student learning so that teachers and the Green Team have an understanding that what is being taught is actually being learned (see Chapter 9 for ideas on student assessment).

- Data collection can include any of these methods: surveys, interviews, projects, presentations, journals, observations or portfolios. The team can then analyze and interpret the collected data. Next steps can be identified that may involve curriculum revision, gathering more materials or talking with experts, sharing findings with school leaders or expanding to other grade levels.

◆ When creating a school-wide project, include evaluation so that you have an understanding of the effectiveness of the project (see Chapter 9 for more details). A subcommittee of the Green Team can gather feedback and assess the effectiveness of the plan.

- Review and revise goals based on feedback and evaluation processes.
- Share goals and how they were measured with school members. For policies to be institutionalized, guidelines should be established for each area of focus, including "sustainable design guidelines, operations and maintenance guidelines, sustainability management guidelines" (Barr et al., 2014, p. 10) as well as health and wellness guidelines. All guidelines should be shared with school members (including the community) with the idea that everyone has a stake in the outcome. To make it easier for community members, "desired conservation behaviors should be clearly communicated, barriers should be removed, and the positive impact should be reported back to occupants" (Barr et al., 2014, p. 10).

◆ Embed the implemented ideas into the school's "mission, vision and core values" (NPBEA, 2015, p. 4). The team should share progress and ideas with school administrators, staff and students and their families and community. A conversation with school stakeholders about how sustainability can be embedded in the school's mission and vision is crucial and will help to solidify investment by all participants. Making sustainability part of the school culture emphasizes an interconnectedness that includes interdisciplinary problem-based learning, open lines of communication among all school members and a vision that is emersed into how the school functions (Warner & Elser, 2015).

◆ Provide an opportunity for students to lead. Students have initiative, excitement and ideas that can be harnessed by the Green Team. Have students problem-solve campus issues, and help them develop initiatives that can make a difference at the school. Peer mentors can support and guide younger students. For example, at Legacy Elementary in Madison, Alabama, the high school students teach lessons to fifth graders during their Big Fish day at the school's Project Pond, one of the largest outdoor classrooms in Alabama. Likewise, the fifth graders (Big Fish) help plan and deliver science lessons to younger students (the Minnows).

   • Another way to involve students in developing self-efficacy and ownership is to include clubs and/or teams that support school processes. For example, Hamilton Southeastern School Corporation in Fishers, Indiana, has student-led projects such as developing vegetable, rain and pollinator gardens, flower beds and trails.

◆ Develop a sense of place for school members. Creating projects that provide a sense of efficacy will help individuals feel like their achievements make a difference. Feeling ownership in the school can be fostered by having school members see themselves as educators and helpers that value a commitment to community.

   • Once the school has focused on integrating sustainability into the curriculum and after-school clubs and supported the development of school-wide sustainability projects, the Green Team, with the support of the administration, could provide a case for a school sustainability coordinator. And if the school district as a whole has been implementing a sustainability program, a sustainability manager that oversees the entire district would be an appropriate next step.

♦ Review the operations and management of facilities with the school plant manager and school principal (see Chapter 6 for more information about managing a green school). The school building should be a place that is not only functional but also "multisensory, accessible and beautiful" (Barr et al., 2014, p. 9). Students, teachers and staff should have a space that reminds them that "learning is important and their community values learning and provides a beautiful place for them to learn" and work (Barr et al., 2014, p. 9).

• Enlist the help of the school plant manager and conduct an energy/aesthetic audit (https://www.nwf.org/Eco-Schools-USA/Pathways/Audit). A school assessment could include physical structure/facilities, natural light, operations, artificial lighting, temperature, food/drink, atmosphere, etc.

> **Eatonville Elementary, Eatonville, Washington, Monroe Elementary, Hinsdale, Illinois and Readington School District, Whitehouse Station, New Jersey Integration of Environmental Concepts**
>
> Eatonville and Monroe Elementary schools and Readington School District have made significant changes to their school vision and core values. Eatonville Elementary overhauled their curriculum to include STEM and sustainability and national park service staff as part of their school team. Monroe Elementary incorporates environmental projects and gardening to bolster student self-esteem and life skills. In the Readington School District, green initiatives permeate their three core goals (inquiry, social awareness and partnerships) through energy savings, promotion of inquisitive learning and student-driven projects.

- • Report findings to the administration with specific requests that support energy efficiency, aesthetic spaces and healthful living.
- ◆ Consider community partnerships that can help support sustainability projects. Many parents are willing to volunteer their time to help with gardening, build a retention wall, plant trees, etc. Some parents also have expertise that could be used on various projects. Also, local businesses, non-profit organizations and universities (if they are nearby) can supply materials, expertise and help to make a connection to the local community.
- ◆ Communicate with other schools and entities that can provide support and resources.
  - • Present your ideas to others at the Green Schools Conference (https://greenschoolsconference.org/), North American Association for Environmental Education conference(https://conference.naaee.org/conference) or other national or international conferences (https://www.theonlygreenlist.com/green_education/green_education_conferences__seminars).

See Figure 3.1 for a step-by-step approach to greening a school.

Team Building

An understanding of how to create a cohesive team that works well together is needed to find, recruit and include enthusiastic team members who are willing to put in the effort to create a successful program. Essentially, this team will be a Community of Practice (CoP), which is a self-organized group of people who are linked by a common concern or an interest in an issue (Wenger et al., 2002). This CoP will require mutual engagement to be able to work together to achieve a specific purpose, which "involves the creation of skills and actions that lead to fulfilling" that purpose (Bahr et al., 2020, p. 62).

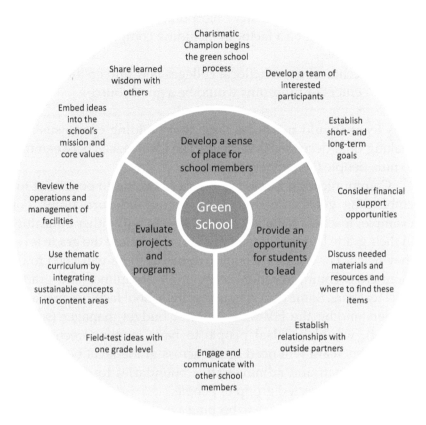

Charismatic Champion begins the green school process

Develop a team of interested participants

Share learned wisdom with others

Establish short- and long-term goals

Embed ideas into the school's mission and core values

Develop a sense of place for school members

Consider financial support opportunities

Review the operations and management of facilities

Green School

Provide an opportunity for students to lead

Use thematic curriculum by integrating sustainable concepts into content areas

Evaluate projects and programs

Discuss needed materials and resources and where to find these items

Field-test ideas with one grade level

Engage and communicate with other school members

Establish relationships with outside partners

FIGURE 3.1 Green Schools step-by-step approach

CREDIT Linda H. Plevyak, PhD

Recruitment from both outside and within the school will make the team more successful. To truly make sustainability an integral part of the school's culture, there should be a broad-based group that includes the following:

- ◆ Educators, staff (including plant manager, custodial and cafeteria staff).
- ◆ Students (if possible).
- ◆ Parents.
- ◆ Community members.
- ◆ Non-profit organizations.

+ Companies/industry (corporate social responsibility [CSR] can be a factor in including companies in greening schools).
+ Technical experts (local colleges and universities, nature centers or museums would be a good source).

This team should not be so large that building consensus and making final decisions is difficult. The ideal size is between five to nine people (Wittenberg, 2006).

Communicating across boundaries is going to be crucial for embedding goals into the school vision and curriculum. For example, teachers have a tendency to talk with other educators in their grade level or, potentially, above or below the grade level they teach. For a green school to succeed, there will need to be more cross communication between all disciplines and grade-level teachers. Some experts, such as the school facilities manager (understanding the HVAC system) or budget manager (school budget), would be ideal people to have on the Green Team. The Green Team will need to cut across grade-level boundaries as well as staff and administrative boundaries to encompass a diverse yet connected group of people.

If there is a reluctance to become a member of the team, there is still the opportunity to gather information and ask questions of experienced school community members. For example, the school facilities manager can provide information and guidance on energy savings and reducing utility costs. Custodians will also be an important resource, and having at least one on the team will be needed as trash, recycling and composting will impact their work. Community members should not be overlooked as there are experienced professionals that will likely be supportive of your efforts. For example, local horticulture experts, such as landscape nursery owners (or specific employees), can help with sustainable landscaping (using native plants) and water conservation.

The Center for Green Schools has a Green Schools Fellowship Program that embeds a fellow for a three-year term to work with school districts so that "change is accelerated in the areas of resource efficiency, improved student health and performance and environmental literacy" (Center for Green Schools, 2018, para. 2). Mainly large urban school districts are the ones that are supported through this program, though school districts that have high-need students will be considered. Each year, five fellows are supported by the Center for Green Schools, and "for a three-year term, the fellow works with the school district to initiate and/or accelerate various initiatives that may have languished for lack of manpower or resources including: monitoring energy usage and decreasing consumption by educating staff and students, etc." (Rainwater & Hartke, 2011, p. 25).

Conclusions

Research has shown that becoming a green school has numerous advantages, including improvement in student academic achievement, improvement of the health and well-being of teachers and students, decreased absenteeism and increased retention rate of teachers. Green schools are also more energy efficient, which saves schools' money, increases engagement with the community and promotes positive environmental behaviors. Being a disadvantaged school is not a barrier to becoming a green school as 50% of the 2012–2014 Green Ribbon award winners had at least 40% of the students qualify for free or reduced lunch. It is typical in a green school to have sustainability initiatives that emphasize student-centered projects, interdisciplinary work and hands-on inquiry. The transformation of poorly used areas into usable green space can help improve the health and well-being of teachers and students. The development of a green school typically starts with one person who has the enthusiasm and drive to create a successful program.

Questions to Consider

♦ Are you considering supporting the green school process at your school, and if so, are you willing to be the Charismatic Champion?

- ◆ What are important things you need to know to begin the green school process?
- ◆ Who at your school would be appropriate Green Team members?
- ◆ What are ways you can convince others to be a part of the Green Team?
- ◆ If you work at a school with a large percentage of free and reduced lunches, what resources will you need to begin the green school development process?
- ◆ Are there outdoor spaces that might be turned into a classroom learning space? If so, what development ideas do you have?

References

Akpinar, A. (2016). How is high school greenness related to students' restoration and health? *Urban Forestry & Urban Greening, 16*, 1–8.

Ardoin, N., Bowers, A., Roth, N., & Holthius, N. (2018). Environmental education and K-12 student outcomes: A review and analysis of research. *Journal of Environmental Education, 49*(1), 1–17.

Bahr, D., Newberry, M., & Rino, J. (2020). Connecting preservice and inservice teacher learning: Communities of practice. *School Science and Mathematics Association, 121*, 61–71.

Bahr, S., & Sparks, D. (2016). *Changes in America's public school facilities: From school year 1998–99 to school year 2012–13*. NCES. https://nces.ed.gov/pubsearch/pubsinfo.asp?pubid=2016074.

Barr, S. K., Cross, J. E., & Dunbar, B. H. (2014). *The whole-school sustainability framework: Guiding principles for integrating sustainability into all aspects of a school organization*. https://www.usgbc.org/education/sessions/whole-school-sustainability-framework-12846102.

Boeve-de Pauw, J., Gericke, N., Olsson, D., & Berlund, T. (2015). The effectiveness of education for sustainable development. *Sustainability, 7*, 15693–15717.

Boeve-de Pauw, J., & Petegem, P. (2013). The effect of eco-schools on children's environmental values and behavior. *Journal of Biological Education, 47*(2), 96–103.

Borg, C., Gericke, N., Höglund, H. O., & Bergman, E. (2012). The barriers encountered by teachers implementing education for sustainable development: Discipline bound differences and teaching traditions. *Research in Science & Technological Education*, *30*(2), 185–207.

Buckley, J., Schneider, M., & Shang, Y. (2005). Fix it and they might stay: School facility quality and teacher retention in Washington, DC. *Teachers College Record*, *107*(5), 1107–1123.

Center for Green Schools. (2018). *Green schools fellowship program*. https://www.centerforgreenschools.org/green-schools-fellowship-program.

Center for Green Schools. (2021). *Every school can be a green school: Getting started checklist*. https://www.centerforgreenschools.org/.

Danks, S. (2021). *Living school grounds*. https://www.greenschoolyards.org/living-school-grounds.

Filardo, M. (2021). *2021 state of our schools: America's PK–12 pubic school facilities*. 21st Century Fund.

Ghent, C., Trauth-Nare, A., Dell, K., & Haines, S. (2014). The influence of a statewide green school initiative on student achievement in K–12 classrooms. *Applied Environmental Education & Communication*, *13*(4), 250–260.

Green Schoolyards America. (2021). *Mission statement*. https://www.greenschoolyards.org/about

Haverinen-Shaughnessy, U., Moschandreas, D. J., & Shaughnessy, R. J. (2011). Association between substandard classroom ventilation rates and students' academic achievement. *Indoor Air*, *21*(2), 121–131.

Hus, J., Qin, X., Beavers, S., & Mirabelli, M. (2016). Asthma-related school absenteeism, morbidity, and modifiable factors. *American Journal of Preventive Medicine*, *51*(1), 23–32.

Hutter, H. P., Haluza, D., Piegler, K., Hohenblum, P., Frohlich, M., & Scharf, S. (2013). Semivolatile compounds in schools and their influence on cognitive performance of children. *International Journal of Occupational Medical and Environmental Health*, *26*(4), 628–635.

Kats, G. (2006). *Greening America's schools: Cost and benefits. A capital E report*. https://www.usgbc.org/resources/greening-america039s-schools-costs-and-benefits.

Laurie, R., Nonoyama-Tarumi, Y., McKeown, R., & Hopkins, C. (2016). Contributions of education for sustainable development (ESD) to quality education: A synthesis of research. *Journal of Education for Sustainable Development, 10*(2), 226–242.

Lieberman, G. (2013). *Education and the environment: Creating standards-based programs in schools and districts.* Harvard Education Press.

Martenies, S. E., & Batterman, S. A. (2018). Effectiveness of using enhanced filters in schools and homes to reduce indoor exposures to PM2.5 from outdoor sources and subsequent health benefits for children with asthma. *Environmental Science & Technology, 52*(18), 10767–10776.

Maryland Association for Environmental and Outdoor Education. (2021). *Green school's program.* https://maeoe.org/green-schools-and-green-centers/green-schools-program.

McKey, T. (2017). *U.S. department of education green ribbon schools award from 2012, 2013, and 2014: Teacher perceptions of ecological and democratic principles.* http://www.susted.com/wordpress/content/u-s-department-of-education-green-ribbon-schools-award-from-2012–2013-and-2014-teacher-perceptions-of-ecological-and-democratic-principles_2017_03/.

Midouhas, E., Kokosi, T., & Flouri, E. (2018). Outdoor and indoor air quality and cognitive ability in young children. *Environmental Research, 161*, 321–328.

Mogren, A., Gericke, N., & Scherp, H. (2019). Whole school approaches to education for sustainable development: A model that links to school improvement. *Environmental Education Research, 25*(4), 508–531.

National Policy Board for Educational Administration. (2015). *Professional standards for educational leaders.* https://www.wallacefoundation.org/knowledgecenter/Documents/Professional-Standards-for-Educational-Leaders-2015.pdf.

Next Generation Science Standards. (2013). *The standards.* https://www.nextgenscience.org/overview-topics.

North American Association for Environmental Education (NAAEE). (2018). *EE provides a wide array of benefits for K-12 students.* https://naaee.org/.

Olsson, D., Gericke, N., & Rundgren, S.-N. (2015). The effect of implementation of education for sustainable development in Swedish compulsory schools: Assessing pupil's sustainability consciousness. *Environmental Education Research*, *22*(2), 176–202.

Plevyak, L., Tamsukhin, S., & Gibson, R. (2019). Building a foundation for sustainable principles: Case studies of K-6 green ribbon schools. *Journal of Sustainability Education*, *21*, 1–19.

Pulimeno, M., Piscitelli, P., Colazzo, S., Colao, A., & Miani, A. (2020). Indoor air quality at school and students' performance: Recommendation of the UNESCO chair on health education and sustainable development & the Italian society of environmental medicine (SIMA). *Health Promotion Perspective*, *10*(3), 169–174.

Rainwater, B., & Hartke, J. (2011). *Local leaders in sustainability: Special report from Sundance (A national action plan for greening America's school)*. The American Institute of Architects and the U.S. Green Building Council, Inc.

Sterrett, W. L., Imig, S., & Moore, D. (2014). U.S. department of education green ribbon schools: Leadership insights and implications. *Journal of Organizational Learning and Leadership*, *12*(2), 1–18.

U.S. EPA. (2020). *Why indoor air quality is important to schools*. https://www.epa.gov/iaq-schools/why-indoor-air-quality-important-schools.

UNICEF. (2021). *Growing cities*. https://childfriendlycities.org/growing-cities/.

Verhelst, D., Vanhoof, J., Boeve-de Pauw, J., & Van Petegem, P. (2020). Building a conceptual framework for an ESD-effective school organization. *The Journal of Environmental Education*, *51*(6), 400–415.

Warner, B. P., & Elser, M. (2015). How do sustainable schools integrate sustainability education? An assessment of certified sustainable K–12 schools in the United States. *Journal of Environmental Education*, *46*(1), 1–22.

Wenger, E., McDermott, R., & Snyder, W. M. (2002). *Cultivating communities of practice: A guide to managing knowledge*. Harvard Business School Press.

Wittenberg, E. (2006). *Is your team too big? Too small? What's the right number?* https://knowledge.wharton.upenn.edu/article/is-your-team-too-big-too-small-whats-the-right-number-2/.

World Health Organization. (2017). *Urban green spaces: A brief for action*. World Health Organization.

4

What Does a Successful Green School Look Like?

"In every walk with nature one receives far more than what he seeks."

John Muir

Vignette

Matt, a junior at Hamilton High School, was trying to figure out what to do for his senior project when he bumped into the environmental science teacher, Ms. Zabor. He was enjoying her class as she had them complete a biodiversity hike at the community nature center. Matt was interested in how non-native plant species were impacting the diversity of plants and animals in the Parker Woods Nature Preserve near his home in south central Ohio. He asked Ms. Zabor if she would help him with his project proposal. She said she would be happy to and that they should meet after class. Matt wanted to research Amur honeysuckle, which is an invasive species and has been found at the Parker Woods Nature Preserve. NASA scientists, using satellite images (https://envirobites. org/2020/09/07/how-to-study-invasive-species-from-space/), studied

DOI: 10.4324/9781003164524-4

the nature preserve in 2015. He was hoping to use the data from the study to compare to the present day and see if there was a difference. Matt really wanted to get an internship with the U.S. Geological Survey group in the summer and thought this project would be a way to make a good impression. He couldn't wait to meet with Ms. Zabor!

Chapter Objectives

- ◆ Highlight how schools are creating an environment for learning.
- ◆ Share the characteristics of a green school.
- ◆ Explain how outdoor space can be used.
- ◆ Discuss how leadership impacts the development and success of a green school.

Creating the Ideal Environment for Learning

Have you ever heard a student ask, "Why are we learning this?" In a conventional school where lecture is the dominant method of teaching and subject areas are taught in silos, students have a difficult time understanding how content is connected or what it means to their own lives. The ideal is for students to not only understand content but also connect it to prior learning and life experiences. Students should also be engaged and enthusiastic about what they are learning. Using sustainability as the underlying theme, teachers can facilitate rather than dictate while students actively make their own discoveries. Green school programs share a philosophy that sustainability should be a whole-school approach (Gough, 2020), providing students with life-building skills such as critical thinking, communication and leadership; social skills such as self-esteem, character development and team work; as well as the ability to resolve conflicts and take action.

Readington Middle School (RMS) is an excellent example, modeling a whole-school sustainability approach. The Coordinator of Green Initiatives and Sustainability, B. Freeman, promotes student-led, inquiry-based learning, research and action. RMS uses the UN Global Goals (2021) as a foundation for projects, with "students identifying problems they see/or experience in their community, connect them to global issues, research, prototype, and develop solutions" (B. Freeman, personal communication, January 12, 2022). For example, in Photo 4.1, students at Readington Middle School are putting together a hydroponic system that will be used to cultivate plants. Students will be studying the nutrients and plant growth over time.

The traditional farming vs. aeroponics vs. aquaponics investigation stemmed from a vertical garden system students had developed that they named FIG (fresh food from indoor gardens). A student presentation of the project was submitted to the ePals-Smithsonian Invent-it Challenge and won. A FIG prototype that the students created is currently on display at the Smithsonian. Photo 4.2 shows the culmination of the

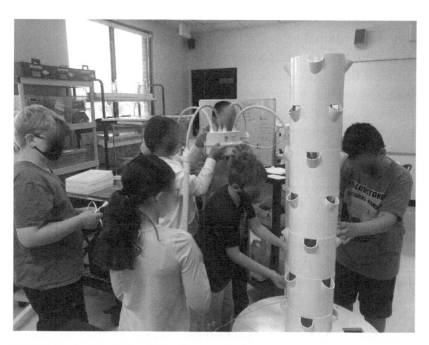

CREDIT Jonathan Hart, PhD and Betsy Freeman, Readington Township Public School District

Readington Middle School students' efforts with the hydroponic system. These greens were harvested before the winter break. As these students live in Whitehouse Station, New Jersey, this is not something that could be accomplished outside. The class discusses food insecurity, what we can do about food waste, the importance of good nutrition and how enjoyable it is to eat fresh greens during the cold winter months. Readington Middle School no longer uses Styrofoam trays in their cafeteria, so they repurposed them to be used in the seed lab. At the end of the investigations, the students donate their fresh greens to the local food bank. The students see what they do as meaningful and also promoting a sense of caring for others at the same time.

Different countries have unique ways of interpreting how to become a green school. In the U.S., school districts are "motivated by the cost savings sustainability programs offer," though schools are also interested in supporting enrichment and the "educational experience" for students (Coyle, 2020, p. 397). Understanding

CREDIT Jonathan Hart, PhD and Betsy Freeman, Readington Township Public School District

how wide-ranging these programs are is difficult as individual states have oversight of education and local public school districts control decisions about facilities and curriculum. The Australia Sustainable Schools Initiative (AuSSI) "integrates existing environmental and social education programs and resources into a coordinated framework" (2016, p. 1) and helps to establish relationships with local communities (Gough, 2020). Taiwan has developed the Greenschool Partnership Network (GPN) with the goal of establishing environmental literacy, greening school campuses, building partnerships (e.g., U.S.–Taiwan Eco-Campus Partnership) and promoting active learning through "humanistic concern" (Gough, 2020, p. 20). In 2016, Germany implemented the German Curricular Framework for the Global Development Learning (OR)/Education for Sustainable Development (ESD) (Elster, 2020). A goal for the 16 federal states of Germany is the integration of ESD and "is oriented to the 'triangle of sustainability' (economic, social and environment) as a holistic development model" (Elster, 2020, pp. 178–179). As of 2018, Eco-Schools is used in 960 German schools (out of approximately 2,500 total schools) (German Way, 2021).

Characteristics of a Green School

As highlighted in other chapters, green schools can be created by emphasizing a diverse set of goals, including a physical plant (reducing environmental impacts and costs), health and wellness and curriculum (environmental and sustainability literacy). The more interconnected the sustainability programs are to the school mission, curriculum, organizations and overall running of the school, the more likely they will be successful (Warner & Elser, 2015).

Physical Plant
Understanding building operations can be intimidating, especially if there is no representation from building management staff on the Green Team (see Chapter 6 as it goes into more details

about managing a green school). There are a couple of options available, including finding a "knowledge broker" (Ishiyama, 2016, p. 1305), someone who has the requisite understanding, either inside or outside the school community. The use of a knowledge broker can be with any needed expertise, including health, curriculum and energy savings. These brokers can be paid or volunteer members of the Green Team and may be only required for a specific period. Having someone from the school's physical plant staff supporting the committee would be the easiest, though if there is reluctance, it might require persuasion through an explanation of goals, how the Green Team efforts could positively impact working conditions or possibly training (which administration would need to support). The second option is to find another school that is further along in developing their sustainability program and learn from their experience.

Having an efficient heating and cooling system will save not only energy but money as well. Schools that don't have the budget to swap out their current system with a more energy-efficient system can still take intermittent steps towards becoming green. For example, smart thermostats can be pre-programmed and controlled from a mobile device. School staff can be notified when temperatures reach a certain level. Typically, these smart thermostats have Energy Star approval and can save approximately 7%–33% on annual energy costs (Kull et al., 2020).

Health and Wellness

Maintaining good physical health allows students and teachers to concentrate on learning. As discussed in Chapter 3, a green school will have a good ventilation system that increases air movement and dilutes or removes pollutants through ventilation, which should reduce flu, headaches and other respiratory problems (Kats, 2006). Safe drinking water is required, preferably with accessible reusable water stations that are cleaned often. Improving classroom acoustics that control for background noise and reverberation will also be a focus of a green school. Using non-toxic paint and carpeting that doesn't release toxic chemicals into the air will support better concentration and health as well.

Along with clean air and water, greening schools creates an opportunity to focus on nutrition, ensuring a healthy diet (see Chapter 8 for more information on this topic). The Center for Green Schools has more than 80 lessons that highlight teaching about food (2017), and the Green School Initiative includes a detailed "directory of resources covering product information for greener food service-ware that is compostable, biodegradable, or has recycled content, as well as information about healthy school lunch and farm-to-school programs" (2021, para. 3).

Mental and emotional health are as important as physical health, though schools may not focus on these aspects as much. With an estimated 20%–25% of K–12 students experiencing a mental health disorder, it is crucial to incorporate support into the school system (Bains & Diallo, 2016). The strong link between mental health and academic performance also requires a need for support (Borntrager & Lyon, 2015). There is a fair amount of ambiguity in how to support students, though an interesting example is Social Emotional Learning (SEL), which focuses on developing self-awareness, self-management, social awareness, relationship skills and responsible decision-making (Hess, 2018). SEL can be defined as,

> the process through which children and adults acquire and effectively apply the knowledge, attitudes, and skills necessary to understand and manage emotions, set and achieve positive goals, feel and show empathy for others, establish and maintain positive relationships, and make responsible decisions. (Collaborative for Academic, Social, and Emotional Learning [CASEL], 2015, para. 1)

SEL has been expanded to include a mindfulness practice that focuses on the well-being of students (as well as teachers and staff), with positive effects (Vickery & Dorjee, 2015). Using a mindfulness practice helps to consider the "whole child" while supporting emotional and social skills (Rempel, 2012). In Photo 4.3, a young student is meditating as part of the Newport School's well-being program, which is integrated across all grade levels and is designed to bring emotional, mind and body balance.

Curriculum

A green school would have the following goals in relation to curriculum: an emphasis on teaching sustainability concepts, promotion of environmental education that is highly interconnected with interdisciplinary problem-based learning, an increase in across-grade-level teacher communication and a change in the vision of education (Warner & Elser, 2015). For this to happen, "anchoring the work in teaching teams" and providing the "development of a professional language and a repertoire of stories, experiences and artifacts" (Madsen, 2013, pp. 3779–3780) is required so that the school community has a foundation on which to build sustainability concepts. Creating a

CREDIT Nathalia Remolina, Colegio Newport

community of practice, where members have a "shared meaning and understanding of a particular topic" and their relationship is "built upon trust and respect" while being "held together by a common body of knowledge," (Hizar Md Khuzaimah & Hassan, 2012, p. 347) will provide support and encouragement when needed.

The curriculum itself should be interdisciplinary and participative and include problem-solving and experiential learning (Moore et al., 2019). The Eco-Schools Pathways has created theme-based focus areas that K–12 schools can follow that include biodiversity, climate change, consumption and waste, energy, healthy living, healthy schools, learning about forests, schoolyard habitats, sustainable food, transportation, water and watersheds, oceans and wetlands (2021). Connecting to the community will strengthen partnerships and allow teachers an opportunity to connect with needed experts. Possible ways to include community members is through field trips, reclaiming riparian habitats, after-school clubs, Earth Day celebrations or hosting a community reuse center.

The Use of Outdoor Space

As the previous section described, going outside not only focuses on the environment but can reduce chronic absenteeism (MacNaughton et al., 2017), improve attention deficit disorder (Schulman & Peters, 2008), increase school performance and positive attitudes about school, improve behavior and develop an appreciation for nature (Lieberman & Hoody, 1998). Another incentive for using the physical environment for learning is that it can cut across all disciplines, including math, science, technology and English (Kerlin et al., 2015). So when thinking about the outdoor space of the school, consider how the building and outdoor environment can play a role in the learning process. An inventory of the school grounds can inform you of existing resources (the school plant manager should be able to help with this process). Take photos of all outdoor learning infrastructure, and complete the Leaf Program Inventory (2012). Once the inventory is completed, in conjunction with the Green Team and the plant manager, weigh the pros and cons of the current outdoor space and develop a plan that includes renovations or adaptations that will promote quality learning experiences.

Part of the school renovation plan could be to consider reducing paved areas (which cuts down on storm runoff) and replacing them with ground cover, native planting or trees. If a large paved space is not being used efficiently, creating a living school area "which is a richly layered outdoor environment that strengthens local ecological systems while providing place-based, hands-on learning resources" (Green Schoolyards America, 2021, para. 1) could be developed. Other outdoor spaces that could be adapted for learning include playgrounds, athletic fields, tracks and landscaped or developed green spaces. For example, tree stumps could be used for seating, or collapsible picnic tables could be stored away if more space is needed. Photos 4.4 and 4.5 show before and after pictures of a parking lot at Colegio Santa Francisca Romana. The after picture shows permeable pavers, which allow rainwater to drain through.

CREDIT Kattia Marcela Lozada Mariño, Colegio Santa Francisca Romana

CREDIT Kattia Marcela Lozada Mariño, Colegio Santa Francisca Romana

How Leadership Can Support the Development and Success of a Green School

Making progress in creating a green school will be realized and sustained if school leadership is supportive (Sterrett & Imig, 2015). The school principal serves as the "critical player in giving direction and focus to the school to bring about learning for *all* students" (Matthews & Crow, 2010, p. 5). Both school administration and teachers can be change agents that seek to incorporate sustainability. Including parents and local community members as partners "will certainly improve the chances of the program producing positive outcomes" (Sterrett et al., 2014, p. 7).

As well, many professional education organizations, state and federal government, and non-profit organizations influence PreK–12 education. These entities develop and implement policy, procedures and research that (hopefully) help to make positive gains in student learning. In relation to green schools,

> there are encouraging signs that many of the major education NGOs in the U.S. are supporting green school

programming. These include: the American Association for the Advancement of Science, the American Federation of Teachers, Association for Supervision and Curriculum Development, the Council of Chief State School Officers, the National Association of Elementary School Principals, the National Association of Secondary School Principals, The National Education Association and others. (Coyle, 2020, pgs. 397–398)

The National Education Association (NEA) is the largest labor union in the U.S., with 3 million members, the American Federation of Teachers (AFT) has 1.7 million members and the American Association for the Advancement of Science (AAAS) has 120,000 members and is the world's largest scientific society (NEA, 2021; AFT, 2021; AAAS, 2021). Having these organizations essentially endorse sustainability in PreK–12 education can provide support for Green Teams at the local level.

The school community is the beneficiary of sustainability efforts and as such should be, as much as possible, a part of the process. Communication via newsletter, email, text or social media can increase motivation and interest. "By inviting the community to be a part of the collaborative process to green a school, and by including them in on-going sustainability initiatives, a green school can become a source of civic pride" (Rainwater & Hartke, 2011, p. 9).

As part of the Green Ribbon Award (ED-GRS), the first pillar focuses on reducing costs, and school leaders can make the case that lessening the environmental impact can save money. For example, Parkway School District in Chesterfield, Missouri, has a Director of Purchasing and Sustainability who values integration and involves students in the sustainability curriculum. One of the school district's partners, the Earthway Center at the Missouri Botanical Gardens, helps the students "understand how their behavior impacts plants and the entire environment" (Missouri Botanical Garden, 2021, para 3). With each of the Parkway schools incorporating solar panels and one high school receiving a geothermal well field, there is a long-term vision within the school district in relation to sustainability.

The second pillar of the ED-GRS emphasizes improving health and wellness so school leaders can focus on reducing absenteeism and obesity with cleaner air and healthy nutrition. For example, at North Park School for Innovation in Columbia Heights, Minnesota, the principal and a science teacher emphasize healthful nutrition with a share table for food in the cafeteria, a courtyard garden with on-site composting and a Tower Hydroponic Garden System in the science lab. The goal at North Park is to improve the nutritional value of food with locally sourced ingredients and the use of scratch cooking. Another example highlights helping students understand the farm-to-table concept as Legacy Elementary in Madison, Alabama, grows radishes, spinach, potatoes, peanuts, cotton and soybean, with students actively engaged with the planting and growing process.

The final pillar of the ED-GRS highlights sustainability education that promotes hands-on, experiential learning. For example, Green Schools International, which includes locations in Bali, Indonesia; Tulum, Mexico; Taranaki, New Zealand; and Cape Town, South Africa, hires teachers that are passionate about the environment and promotes mental, social and physical health in all of their schools. The schools take a thematic approach to the sustainable development goals and culminates with a student-led project. They also support each local community by focusing on special programs, including seed to table. With each of these examples, the leadership came from a diverse set of people, including a sustainability coordinator, a head of teaching and learning, administration, teachers and staff (cafeteria and physical plant).

Conclusions

The main goals of green schools is to teach students to be problem solvers, lifelong learners and passionate community leaders. Incorporating sustainability into this goal is a whole school endeavor and, as such, requires team work and good communication. Developing a Green Team that includes representatives from the building and cafeteria management who are willing to support sustainability measures will help to ensure a successful green school. Good nutrition and the maintenance of physical health allows students and teachers to achieve increased performance. The well-being of students' mental and emotional health is also crucial as there is a strong link between mental health and academic success. Spending time outside can support students through behavior improvement, reducing absenteeism, maintaining a positive attitude about school and developing an appreciation for nature. School leadership is needed to make advances on green school initiatives. When teachers, parents and community members collaborate on these initiatives, the green school can become the pride of the local community.

Questions to Consider

- ◆ What are the main goals of your school?
- ◆ How do these goals get implemented?
- ◆ What are three ways that student physical, mental and emotional health can be supported at your school?
- ◆ How might you increase the time that students spend outside? What type of learning experiences could occur outdoors at your school?
- ◆ Which school staff members might be open to supporting green school initiatives?

References

American Association for the Advancement of Science. (2021). *Advancing, science, engineering and innovation*. www.aaas.org/

American Federation of Teachers. (2021). *American federation of teachers*. www.aft.org/

Australian Sustainable Schools Initiative. (2016). *AuSSI*. A practical guide to the Australian Sustainable Schools Initiative in Western Australia.

Bains, R. M., & Diallo, A. F. (2016). Mental health services in school-based health centers: A systematic review. *The Journal of School Nursing*, *32*(1), 8–19.

Borntrager, C., & Lyon, A. R. (2015). Client progress monitoring and feedback in school-based mental health. *Cognitive and Behavioral Practice, 22*(1), 74–86.

Center for Green Schools. (2017). *3 lessons on nutrition for K–12 students.* www.centerforgreenschools.org/3-lessons-nutrition-k%E2%80%9312-students

Collaborative for Academic, Social, and Emotional Learning. (2015). *What is social and emotional learning?* www.casel.org/social-and-emotional-learning.

Coyle, K. J. (2020). Green schools in the United States. In A. Gough & N. Gough (Eds.), *Green schools globally, international explorations in Outdoor and environmental education* (pp. 385–401). Springer.

Eco-Schools Pathways. (2021). *Pathways to sustainability.* www.nwf.org/Eco-Schools-USA/Pathways

Elster, D. (2020). Eco-Schools movement in Germany in the light of educational reforms. In A. Gough & N. Gough (Eds.), *Green schools globally, international explorations in Outdoor and environmental education* (pp. 169–188). Springer.

Germany Way. (2021). *The German school system.* www.german-way.com/history-and-culture/education/the-german-school-system/

Gough, A. (2020). Seeking a green future through education. In A. Gough & N. Gough (Eds.), *Green schools globally, international explorations in outdoor and environmental education* (pp. 13–29). Springer.

Green Schools Initiative. (2021). *Green food services, healthy lunch, and farm to table.* www.greenschools.net/display.php-modin=54&uid=58.html

Green Schoolyards America. (2021). *Living school grounds.* www.greenschoolyards.org

Hess, L.B. (2018). *Mindfulness in K-12 education: A case study approach exporing the implementation and sustainability of school mindfulness programs.* [Unpublished doctoral disseration]. Boston University.

Hizar Md Khuzaimah, K., & Hassan, F. (2012). Uncovering tacit knowledge in construction theory: Communities of practice approach. *Procedia – Social and Behavioral Sciences, 50,* 343–349.

Ishiyama, N. (2016). Role of knowledge brokers in communities of practice in Japan. *Journal of Knowledge Management, 20*(6), 1302–1317.

Kats, G. (2006). *Greening America's schools: Cost and benefits. A capital E report.* www.usgbc.org/resources/greening-america039s-schools-costs-and-benefits

Kerlin, S., Santos, R., & Bennett, W. (2015). Green schools as learning laboratories? Teachers' perceptions of their first year in a new green middle school. *Journal of Sustainability Education*, *8*.

Kull, T. M., Penu, K. R., Thalfeldt, M., & Kurnitski, J. (2020). *Energy saving potential with smart thermostats in low-energy homes in cold climate.* Web of Conferences, 172, Smart Thermostats and Energy Saving Potential.

Leaf Program Inventory. (2012). *Leaf school grounds development handbook.* School Grounds Inventory.

Lieberman, G. A., & Hoody, L. L. (1998). *Closing the achievement gap: Using the environment as an integrating context for learning.* SEER.

MacNaughton, P., Eitland, E., Kloog, I., Schwartz, J., & Allen, J. (2017). Impact of particulate matter exposure and surrounding "greenness" on chronic absenteeism in Massachusetts public schools. *International Journal of Environmental Research and Public Health*, *14*(2), 207.

Madsen, K. (2013). Unfolding education for sustainable development as didactic thinking and practice. *Sustainability*, *5*(9), 3771–3782.

Matthews, L. J., & Crow, G. M. (2010). *The principalship: New roles in a professional learning community.* Allyn and Bacon.

Missouri Botanical Gardern. (2021). *EarthWays center.* www.missouribotanicalgarden.org/sustainability/sustainability/about-sustainability.aspx

Moore, M., O'Leary, P., Sinnott, D., & Russell O'Connor, J. (2019). Extending communities of practice: A partnership model for sustainable schools. *Environment Development and Sustainability*, *21*, 1745–1762.

National Education Association. (2021). *Purpose and power in the community.* www.nea.org/

Rainwater, B., & Hartke, J. (2011). *Local leaders in sustainability: Special report from Sundance (A national action plan for greening America's school).* The American Institute of Architects and the U.S. Green Building Council, Inc.

Rempel, K. D. (2012). Mindfulness for children and youth: A review of the literature with an argument for school-based implementation. *Canadian Journal of Counselling & Psychotherapy*, *46*, 201–220.

Schulman, A., & Peters, C. A. (2008). GIS analysis of urban schoolyard landcover in three U.S. cities. *Urban Ecosystems, 11*(1), 65–80.

Sterrett, W. L., & Imig, S. (2015). Learning green: Perspectives from U.S. Department of Education green ribbon schools educators. *Journal of Sustainability Education, 10.*

Sterrett, W. L., Imig, S., & Moore, D. (2014). U.S. Department of education green ribbon schools: Leadership insights and implications. *Journal of Organizational Learning and Leadership, 12*(2), 1–18.

United Nations Global Goals. (2021). *The global goals for sustainable development.* www.globalgoals.org/

Vickery, C. E., & Dorjee, D. (2015). Mindfulness training in primary schools decreases negative affect and increases meta-cognition in children. *Frontiers in Psychology, 6,* 2025.

Warner, B. P., & Elser, M. (2015). How do sustainable schools integrate sustainability education? An assessment of certified sustainable K-12 schools in the United States. *Journal of Environmental Education, 46*(1), 1–22.

5

Teaching Project- and Problem-Based Learning in a Green School

"If all mankind were to disappear, the world would regenerate back to the rich state of equilibrium that existed ten thousand years ago. If insects were to vanish, the environment would collapse into chaos."

E.O. Wilson

Vignette

School had let out for the day, though in one of the high school social studies classrooms at Roosevelt Middle School (RMS), quite a bit of commotion could be heard emanating down the hall. There were fifth and sixth grade students moving desks in a circle while Ms. Williford organized clipboards and evaluation forms. She looked up to watch the students and contemplated the last few years with the Climate Crew, an after-school club that had developed out of the sustainability committee – a group of teachers, staff and administrators at RMS that were focused on cutting down on energy use and using renewable energy when possible. It had all started with the Whole School

DOI: 10.4324/9781003164524-5

Sustainability Framework (Barr et al., 2014) from the Center for Green Schools at the U.S. Green Building Council in collaboration with the Institute for the Built Environment. When a few teachers at Roosevelt Elementary were looking for guidance on how to save energy, the framework became a good resource on how to create a vision for the school. As Ms. Williford thought about the evolution of the committee and the advances the school had made, she smiled and moved towards the circle of chairs the student had made, realizing that she was excited about the energy audit they were going to conduct that afternoon.

Chapter Objectives

- Discuss how to teach in a school that emphasizes sustainable practices.
- Connect inquiry-based and project- and problem-based (real-world) learning to green school practices.
- Explain how to focus learning on the student, emphasizing experiential learning.

Teaching in a Green School

Teaching is one of the most challenging careers that a person can undertake. It requires organization, thoughtful analysis of the target audience, an understanding of human development and pedagogical approaches, reflection on practice, expert content knowledge, patience and enthusiasm. It is also an incredibly rewarding career as teachers help to shape future generations of world citizens. Teachers who listen to students and observe them carefully understand what the students already know (and don't know), which helps to build an understanding of the next steps. The traditional approach to teaching, where instructors use lecture, has been shown to be an efficient way to cover large chunks of content quickly (Omelicheva & Avdeyeva, 2008). However, this efficiency is also its downfall as it does not foster the important critical thinking and analysis required for long-term retention (Green & Dorn, 1999). Also, while the lecture happens, students are passive learners who are not typically engaging their emotions, which is required for effective learning to take place (Brandt, 1998). For students to learn and retain new ideas, they need to relate information to what they have learned previously and then transfer that information to their long-term memory. As Figure 5.1 shows, we interpret the environment using our five senses, with some items registering only in our short-term memory (e.g., phone numbers, passwords and people's names) then quickly forgotten.

To have a chance of retaining content, the information has to make it into our working memory, where meaning making occurs and where we make sense of the information prior to storing it in long-term memory. Once content is in the long-term memory, we link the content with other information we have learned over our lifetime (Varga & Bauer, 2017). An important, meaningful experience is retained for longer periods, which "requires more information in storage" and the ability to recall the content from a previous "learning event" (Haist, Shimamura, & Squire, p. 691). Let's try this out in real time and see how it relates to your own life. Think about what you

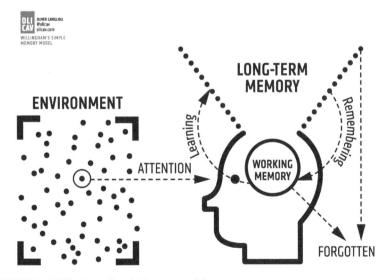

FIGURE 5.1 Willingham's Simple Memory model

CREDIT Oliver Caviglioli

did last Friday night. Do you recall what you had for dinner or the events of the evening? This is likely not something that you retain in your long-term memory as it wasn't important or meaningful. Now, think about one event you remember from this past month. Why do you think you remember that particular event? Was it a celebration or someone's birthday, a meaningful experience that engaged your emotions? If so, it will likely be retained in your memory as it links to other meaningful events in your life. Now, think about how you can help students retain information that you teach them. Engaging students in meaningful experiences will require going beyond lecture and memorization.

Teaching in a green school is one way to engage students in meaningful experiences as it focuses on using the Environment as an Integrating Context (EIC) for learning. The EIC uses "integrated, interdisciplinary instruction, community-based investigations, collaborative instruction, learner-centered, constructivist approaches, a combination of independent and cooperative learning and local natural surroundings" (State Education and Environment Roundtable, 2013, para. 1).

In a review of research articles over a 20-year period, Stanford University researchers found that teaching about the environment "increases academic performance, enhances critical thinking skills, and helps to develop life-building skills, including confidence, autonomy and leadership" (NAAEE, 2018, para. 2). The EIC model breaks down the boundaries between disciplines and adapts learning to the unique needs and abilities of individual students.

There are a couple of ways to broach incorporating EIC into PreK–12 teaching. One of the successful ways that EIC has been found to work is within the framework of a teacher's own discipline. So if a teacher is licensed in middle school math, they would begin with the math framework and incorporate specific EIC concepts where appropriate. For example, in relation to data sets and dependent and independent variables, students could monitor paper waste in the school and collect data each day for a week (except for one day). The students are then tasked with providing a prediction of the missing entry. They could also graph the data and look for different patterns. Either the teacher or the students could make the decision about what data to gather. Once the students have completed the task, they could broaden the investigation by reviewing how much paper is used throughout the school (collect data, predict, graph and look for patterns) and whether there are opportunities to reduce this amount. Photo 5.1 shows students collecting gray water to be used to water indoor and outdoor plants. The students also keep data on how many liters are being reused.

Another way to incorporate EIC into the classroom is through the holistic approach where the focus is thematic and "issues are addressed in active learning situations where students seek information by themselves and mainly work

CREDIT Jeff Cacek, Stan Mraz, North Park School for Innovation

in groups" (Borg et al., 2012, p. 188) while incorporating content areas relevant to the issue. At the beginning, teachers can provide simple investigations that work through the steps but don't require much data collection, analysis or evaluation. Once students feel comfortable with the process, more complex investigations that use critical thinking skills can be added. When incorporating outdoor experiences in either the content-focused or holistic, theme-based approach, not only will the learning experience be enhanced, but also, students will retain content in long term memory, increase their motivation to learn and enhance or develop positive attitudes towards the environment (Farmer et al., 2007).

An example of project-based sequencing that could be adapted for both the content-focused or holistic, theme-based approach is highlighted here:

- ◆ Introduction/Engagement
  - Introduce the project by engaging the students through a short activity, discussion, video or with a guest speaker. The use of storytelling is one way to introduce an investigation and get students excited and interested. For example, if the project is based on a community issue, students can be told a story about a vacant lot that is near the school that has sat empty for years. Photos can be shown to the students, along with a map of the local area. Their task is to consider the best use of the lot and how it would fit with the neighborhood.
- ◆ Identifying the Problem
  - Example PreK–12 investigation questions based on the Eco-Schools Pathways to Sustainability (2021):
    - Biodiversity
- ◆ How are paved school surfaces currently used? How does the current pavement impact water runoff, pooling or evaporation? Are there paved or unpaved school areas that aren't being used effectively? If so, how can they become a habitat for pollinators (using native plants) and an outdoor classroom for environmental investigations?
  - Climate Change

- How can the school make strides to become a new zero-carbon space?
  - Consumption and Waste
- What happens to the trash that is produced at the school and how can it be decreased?
- How can leftover food or food waste be used? How can composting be incorporated into the school cafeteria?
  - Energy
- How efficient is the school furnace? Are there other renewable energy sources that could be used?
- How could a rooftop garden, tree canopy or living wall help to offset heating and cooling needs?
- Where does light enter the school building? How can natural lighting be incorporated into classrooms, cafeteria and other used spaces?
- What is the temperature near school windows vs. the interior of building? Is there a way to efficiently insulate windows, doors and indoor spaces?
- What materials comprise school walls/floors, and are they efficient insulators? If not, are there other environmentally appropriate materials that can be used?
  - Healthy Living
- How does the current school food menu promote fresh, local and nutritious food? Are there potential ways to improve it?
- How is air filtered in the school building? What is the current rate of absenteeism for students and staff, and how much does asthma impact this percentage?
  - Healthy Schools
- How could the current cleaning supplies be improved so that toxins are decreased?
- What is the current absentee rate for students and teachers, and could it be improved by incorporating better air flow, using less toxic cleaning supplies, decreasing idling traffic or using organic pest management?
- How does school traffic flow for drop-off and pickup impact car and bus idling?
  - LEAF

◆ After conducting a schoolyard audit (https://www.nwf.org/Eco-Schools-USA/Pathways/Audit), how can the current (and future) trees help with energy efficiency and provide shade for play and aesthetics of the school grounds?

◆ How does the temperature around the school fluctuate from sun-exposed spaces vs. under a canopy of trees? How does this impact student play?

  • Schoolyard Habitats

◆ Review the completed schoolyard audit and create a design for an outdoor learning space, a pollinator garden and a potential bee apiary. How can the design be implemented?

  • Sustainable Food

◆ How can the cafeteria staff be supported to bring in local, organic food that students and staff enjoy?

◆ How can a school garden be used to supplement students access to fruits and vegetables?

  • Transportation

◆ How do students and staff use transportation to get to school?

◆ How can the use of walking, biking and other efficient types of transportation be increased?

  • Water

◆ Conduct a water audit to answer the following questions (https://www.nwf.org/Eco-Schools-USA/Pathways/Audit):

  • How much water is currently used to flush a toilet in the school?

  • How many sinks and water faucets are there, and are any leaking or in need to repair?

  • What water reduction would be appropriate, both economically and environmentally?

◆ Planning the Approach

  • Students need to consider "the underlying social, political and economic structures and how they contribute to an environmental issue" (Birdsall, 2010,

p. 70). This would include learning *about* action and how to achieve the goals that are set.

- This is also a time to review what students do and don't understand about the environmental issue.
- Develop investigations that are open-ended so that students retain a high level of autonomy in their decision-making.

◆ Research and Analysis

- Students can work independently or in groups towards specific objectives that highlight the issue.
- They can discuss how to broach the issue by learning about who the issue impacts and at what level it resides – school, community, city, state, national or international. Students can also research whether non-profits, businesses or the government may be aligned or have an interest in the issue.
- Next, they can research the issue, gather and analyze the data and interpret its significance in resolving the issue.
- Once all research is completed and students have analyzed the data, decision-making will need to follow. As decision-making is complex and many factors will impact the process, students will need to negotiate with each other (and other groups that can help support the process) about the next steps. Teachers will need to help students with how to see alternative solutions and deal with conflicting opinions (Berglund & Gericke, 2016).

◆ Implementation

- This is a time for students to use the completed research to focus on how to effect change and the direction of said change, which includes the development of a vision as to what needs to be accomplished. This is a crucial step as students are learning *through* action, which helps them to see the culmination of their efforts thus far.
- In relation to the environment, taking action would focus on minimizing our negative impact on the

natural and built world. This behavior can be a direct action, such as cleaning waste from a tributary or an indirect action that influences others through emails or sharing on social media.

- Have students present ideas to a board or group of people who can either provide input or make a decision about the issue. Students can also send emails or letters to appropriate parties as well. If implementation isn't possible or will be delayed, have students develop scenarios as to how they believe the investigation could be concluded. For example, an investigation into a nearby water tributary showed that erosion was occurring, and the students decided that a riparian wall was needed but they might need to wait until spring before future steps could be taken.

◆ Evaluating the Solution
- Throughout the investigation, students should reflect on their current understanding, what is confusing or requires more investigation and what next steps need to be taken. Lastly, students learn *from* action, which includes reflecting on what actions were taken and the ramifications of those actions.
- Teachers can observe student knowledge and understanding, observation, communication, negotiation and social skills and effort and forward progress.

Students' understanding of a subject, especially one that is as complex and value driven as the environment, is tied to their emotions (Manni et al., 2013). As such, "the ethical dimension and emotional aspect of environmental issues is to be taken seriously when teaching Education for Sustainable Development" (Manni et al., 2013, p. 29). The United Nations Educational, Scientific and Cultural Organization (UNESCO, 2021) developed Education for Sustainable Development (ESD) and includes the 17 Sustainable Development Goals (SDGs), which emphasize environmental, political and economic challenges. The EIC and ESD are very similar in that they both focus on empowering the learner to make informed decisions about the environment. ESD does include three more teaching strategies: storytelling, values education and appropriate assessment that can be integrated with the EIC model (Moore et al., 2019).

As we now have an understanding that engaging students in meaningful experiences supports long-term memory retention, it is important to focus on the process of teaching in a green school. There is general agreement by leaders and researchers in education on a body of knowledge that supports the practice of teaching. Teachers will certainly need to use their understanding of students to make informed decisions, though teachers should "align their decisions with the education profession's best understanding of how students learn" (Deans for Impact, 2015, p. 2). These bulleted points are not only beneficial within a green school but could also apply to all PreK–12 teaching.

Vienna International School (VIS) Vienna, Austria Promoting Sustainable Lifestyles through SDGs

The VIS school is the first Eco-School International in Austria and continues to work hard to "build Eco-Bridges" to other schools to join the effort for a sustainable planet. The ESD-School Coordinator meets every week with the Green Teams to organize projects, such as saving energy and water, recycling food waste and protecting local pollinators. The school uses the Outdoor Learning Gardens as a place to promote critical thinking skills and connection to the natural environment. VIS has joined the UNESCO "Trash Hack Campaign," which includes recycling, not using single-use plastic items (straws, cups, bags, etc.) and restoring the planet.

◆ As students learn new information, teachers can refer to ideas they have learned previously. Students will also remember what is being learned if they are given opportunities to "practice retrieving it from their long-term memories and thinking about its meaning" (Deans for Impact, 2015, p. 4). For example, have the students explain a task or process, such as how erosion impacts streams and rivers.

- ◆ Tying meaning to information will help in retaining the content. Using stories or asking students to organize material can help focus attention (McDaniel et al., 1994; Rosenshine et al., 1996).

- ◆ Use a sequenced curriculum that once committed to long-term memory can enable students to develop and retain problem-solving skills (Ericsson et al., 1993).

- ◆ Clear and specific feedback that focuses on the task, not the student, can help move students forward in their learning (Hattie & Timperley, 2007). For example, the teacher can inquire or reflect on a student's effort by stating, "Have you considered how wind and waves impact erosion?"

- ◆ To think critically, students need the knowledge and context to understand a problem's underlying structure (Pellegrino & Hilton, 2012). It might be helpful when solving problems for students to label substeps in a multistep process. For example, students could "trace the energy in the food they eat for lunch back to the sun" (NAAEE, 2019. p. 24).

- ◆ Praise productive student effort, and encourage them to set learning goals. The goal is to develop self-determined motivation rather than motivation based on rewards and punishment (Burnette et al., 2013).

- ◆ Develop an environment where students feel they are accepted and belong (Yeager et al., 2013).

- ◆ Teachers that focus on best practices and recognize common misconceptions of cognitive science will be able to provide their students a high quality of instruction (Pashler et al., 2008; Willingham, 2008).

These bulleted points focus on some of the more important aspects that teachers can implement in a green school classroom to support and guide student learning. In combination with the instructional strategies emphasized in the EIC approach, teachers can have more academically motivated students with increased engagement, reduced classroom management problems and higher scores on standardized measures of academic achievement in reading, writing, math, science and social studies (Lieberman, 2013). Photo 5.2 shows a collaborative effort between Fishers Junior High School students in the Hamilton Southeastern School District, Indiana Department of Natural Resources and the U.S. Forest Service to plant 245 saplings to help save the American Chestnut tree.

Integrating Inquiry and Problem-Based Learning with Green School Practices

An argument that tends to occur when talking about integrating another content area into the PreK–12 curriculum is that there

CREDIT Bob Rice, Hamilton Southeastern School Corporation

is already too much being included and there isn't room for more. This discussion is typically with school boards, politicians, administrators and some teachers who view teaching in a traditional manner with siloed content areas that are taught at specified times throughout the day. Although, integrating the curriculum "more closely resembles how we live and work in the real world" (Kotar et al., 1998, p. 43), which means the curriculum should be organized around what is significant to students, allowing the integration of ideas and concepts into their schemes of meaning. When considering an integrated, inquiry-based curriculum, many subject areas can be taught at one time through a thematic approach to teaching.

Integrating content is the first step in creating a curriculum that focuses on students' experiences while still incorporating a standards-based rigor. The second step is emphasizing problem-based learning (PBL), which can be traced back to John Dewey and his observations of the benefits of hands-on, student-directed experiential learning. One of the explicit goals for learning should be developing and implementing solutions to real problems. PBL highlights an issue or problem and requires students to use their existing knowledge to research, ask questions and interpret information and data to generate plausible solutions. This type of learning typically requires students to use a new perspective or a divergent way of thinking when looking for a solution to a problem. PBL also helps train students to be more open to new ideas, remain curious and ask questions. These skills allow them to make informed decisions based on research and data gathering. As such, the integration of sustainability with other content standards is a valid and accessible instructional strategy.

For example, the Next Generation of Science Standards (NGSS) were introduced in 2013, with a focus on science, technology, engineering and mathematics (STEM) content areas. NGSS also includes science and engineering practices, with an expectation that students will not only "learn content, but understand the methods of scientists and engineers" (NGSS, 2013, para. 2). Approximately 40 states have shown an interest in using the standards, though 20 states, which cover 35% of the students in the U.S., are currently implementing NGSS (2013). The standards "focus more on the place of STEM education in the context of the Earth and its resources and thus emphasize learning science in a broad context" (Coyle, 2020, p. 397). There is a close fit between the environment, energy and natural resources and STEM education, which makes incorporating NGSS in a green school even easier. For example, within the NGSS, each grade level emphasizes some aspect of the environment. These are some examples that incorporate NGSS standards and promote sustainability concepts:

◆ Design a green roof that incorporates a watering system.
◆ Research different types of renewable energy for either a home or school. Collect data on efficiency, cost and amount of space required.
◆ Study the different types of insecticides and fertilizer used by farms. Develop an argument for sustainable ways farmers could control insects and cultivate their crops.

Each NGSS standard comes with ideas of how to implement the standard, ways to develop science and engineering practices, discipline-specific ideas and connections to other content standards such as English or literacy. Numerous states and www.nextgenscience.org have also created a quality curriculum that emphasizes a theme-based approach to teaching the standards. The North American Association for Environmental Education (NAAEE) developed the K–12 Environmental Education: Guidelines for Excellence, which shares a "framework for environmental education programs and curricula, setting a standard for what an environmentally literate person should know" (2019, p. 8).

Of the 50 U.S. states, 41 of them (including the District of Columbia), four U.S. territories and the Department of Defense Education Activity have adopted the Common Core State Standards (CCSS) for math and English language arts, or ELA (as of 2021). In relation to math, the National Council of Teachers of Mathematics (NCTM) has established K–12 content and process standards that describe what math concepts and skills prekindergarten through grade 12 students should know (NCTM, 2000). The content standards include numbers and operations, algebra, geometry, measurement and data analysis and probability. The process standards include problem-solving, reasoning and proof, communication, connections and representation. A connection between the CCSS math standards and sustainability include the following:

♦ Students could calculate the area where an energy system resides (e.g., solar panels on the roof). If there is no renewable energy system at the school, students could review the school energy bill and kilowatt-hour use and then calculate the space where the renewable energy system would reside, producing 25%, 50% or 100% of the school's energy needs. Students could also communicate these findings through a school newsletter or a presentation to administration.

♦ Design a small community that incorporates sustainable concepts such as renewable energy, green spaces, community gardens/compost sites, bike paths and pedestrian-friendly spaces.

♦ Use systems thinking to better understand an environmental issue such as clean water, insecticides, energy use or waste reduction. For example, students could collect data on different types of pesticides and the insects that have developed resistance to them. These data could be graphed and analyzed.

♦ Work through a simulation model using an online climate change solutions tool (https://www. climateinteractive.org/tools/en-roads/), or research a tragedy of the commons concept such as coffee consumption or overfishing (https://online.hbs.edu/blog/post/tragedy-of-the-commons-impact-on-sustainability-issues).

The ELA/literacy standards emphasize an interdisciplinary approach that highlights students' "ability to gather comprehend, evaluate, synthesize, and report on information and ideas, [and] to conduct original research in order to answer questions or solve problems" (CCSS, 2010, para. 6). In conjunction with science, social studies, technology and the arts, ELA provide teachers an excellent opportunity to develop ELA/literacy skills through a problem-based environmental investigation. For example, students can build knowledge, develop vocabulary, gain insights and broaden their perspective about specific environmental issues by reading fiction and non-fiction books. In researching the problem, students can write logical arguments based on substantive claims, which is one of the CCSS objectives for writing. To support speaking and listening CCSS ELA standards, students can participate in group conversations or present their ideas through informal and formal presentations. For example, if students are investigating how to incorporate more green building components into the school, they could present their findings to the school administration, which emphasizes analyzing complex ideas and the collection and evaluation of data. These examples from science, math and ELA can help to support teachers who teach in siloed content areas (that is, teach only one subject area, which is typical in middle and high schools). Other content areas such as social studies (https://www.socialstudies. org/standards), arts education (Arts Education Standards and 21st Century Skills), technology (https://www.iste.org/iste-standards), financial literacy (https://www.councilforeconed. org/resource/national-standards-for-financial-literacy/) and physical education (https://www.shapeamerica.org/ standards/pe/) can also be integrated with environment-based investigations. For example, in Photo 5.3, Hamilton South Eastern students are making observations about their five senses in a natural setting.

If a school is being renovated or a new school that follows LEED standards is being built, teachers have a unique opportunity to use these green infrastructure features in their instruction. When the outdoors is part of an investigation, using a site that is familiar to the students will help to support higher student learning (Bodzin, 2008; Fisman, 2005), though novel experiences can "increase mindfulness and a readiness to learn" (Dale, 2019, p. 8). There are numerous benefits to taking students outside,

CREDIT Bob Rice, Hamilton Southeastern School Corporation

including an increase in cognitive performance, attention span (Wells, 2000), enthusiasm and calm energy; the development of a positive sense of aliveness (Ryan et al., 2010) and the enhancement of a positive relationship with nature (Maller, 2009). Immersive, hands-on, sensory-based experiences, especially at the middle school level, is how students learn best in the outdoors (White & Stoeklin, 2008).

Inquiry- and problem-based education is typically associated with integrating curriculum as it focuses on answering real-world questions and addressing issues that matter to students (Webber & Miller, 2016). For example, at North Park School for Innovation in Columbia Heights, Minnesota, there was major rainwater runoff on a concreted area of the school grounds.

This could be an opportunity for the students to launch an inquiry on how to either capture or divert the rainwater (science), study the volume of rainwater (math), research school historical records as to what was there previously (social studies), present findings to school administration (public speaking, confidence development, delivery, communication) and potential fundraising through grant writing (writing skill, organization, persistence). Involving students in this type of integrated problem-solving allows for engaging, direct experience that promotes civic participation and an ethic of environmental stewardship (Smith & Sobel, 2010). The goal is to connect students to the broader world around them while building an understanding of place and community.

Odyssey Charter School Wilmington, Delaware
Inquiry as Part of a Healthy Lifestyle

Odyssey Charter HS promotes inquiry learning through healthful diets and promoting physically active lives. The school uses the LIFE Curriculum Series, a science and nutrition education program from Teachers College, Columbia University. Students also engage with the large vegetable garden and harvest the produce for both the school cafeteria and local food closet. Environmental advocacy is promoted, with students testifying in favor of a bill to greatly reduce the consumption of single-use plastic bags.

This type of problem-based learning does require planning and organization, which may be difficult for some teachers. If incorporating projects that include unknown outcomes (e.g., projects that may include solving problems) is new to you, it would be helpful to find a mentor or a supportive community of practice that can guide your efforts. There are K–12 forums that support environmental education, including the NAAEE forum https://naaee.org/eepro/groups/k-12-ee and the Education Forum (https://educationforum.ipbhost.com/).

Using PBL in as natural a setting as possible will help to make the issue real for students. For example, a school in an urban setting may have little natural outdoor space for play or investigation. Students could research the surrounding neighborhood and highlight existing gardens, lots and parks that have potential for use. An opportunity to create or support a green space with assistance from a non-profit organization or city park employees could help students to develop communication skills and an awareness and understanding of their neighborhood and promote a sense of belonging. This experience can also be partnered with storytelling, which helps cultivate a sense of place and builds community.

Student-Centered, Experiential Learning

Louv, the author of the book *Last Child in the Woods*, believes that students need outdoor experiences to promote their "ability to learn and think, expand their senses, and improve their physical and mental health" (2012, p. 283). Using the local environment as a place to learn increases students' motivation to learn (Lieberman, 2013) and helps to show students that what they are learning is relevant to the community as well as themselves. There is also an opportunity for teachers to tailor learning to students' experiences. "Teachers at green schools can use the building and the grounds as the basis for project-based, experiential learning. Green schools provide a clear opportunity to connect students with curricula in environmental and STEM education and can serve as a tool for interactive lessons" (Rainwater & Hartke, 2011, p. 9).

Experiential learning uses life experience to construct knowledge and solve learning problems through the experience gained (Kolb, 2014). Experiential learning can support students in the cyclical transition from abstract to concrete action and back again (Shu-Chen et al., 2019). Figure 5.2 shows experiential learning as a feedback loop that begins with experience and uses reflection as an evaluation process, which connects to the action taken. As students complete learning tasks, they are gaining problem-solving competence, making new discoveries and enhancing their comprehension (Sung et al., 2019). The ideal is for students to be self-directed, with internal motivation that comes from their interest in the subject matter. An increase in student self-efficacy

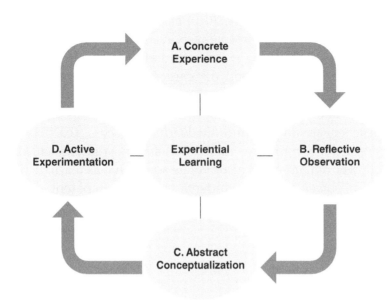

FIGURE 5.2 An experiential learning approach

CREDIT Gwo-Jen Hwang

during the experiential learning process has been shown as students are directly utilizing what they are learning and getting immediate feedback as to the success or failure of the process (Manolis et al., 2013).

An example of experiential learning, using the school building as the focus, would be to better understand how the school's energy system works and see if there are ways to make it more efficient. Students could collect data on hourly or daily energy usage, comparing early morning to late afternoon or weekday vs. weekend energy output. Students could also make predictions of energy usage based on weather forecasts and calculate the CO_2 emissions saved (if the school is using an energy-efficient system such as geothermal or solar panels). A monitoring system or an application that hooks into the system would be the easiest way to review data. Another opportunity that supports students' readiness to learn and promotes student effort and personal responsibility is to incorporate gardening into the school's curriculum

(Royal Horticulture Society, 2010) as it can help with resiliency and the promotion of personal responsibility.

This type of learning is "transformative, where the learning is holistic, open-ended and the students are encouraged to be autonomous" (Birdsall, 2010, p. 71). Students are interdependent, so cooperation and negotiation (with other students as well as the teacher) are important to the learning process. Teachers will need to remain vigilant as motivation among students will vary. The power dynamic will also change somewhat as teachers need to share power with the students and be transparent in how decisions are made.

Conclusions

Many students are still being taught using low levels of learning, such as memorizing and understanding. Learning has to move to the use of critical thinking, including the application of content to novel situations. Many teachers may be unsure how to transition to using problem-based learning that integrates the curriculum, though quality professional development or reaching out to experienced teachers through forum can help the process. Good teaching requires a number of skills, including understanding students, being able to implement a variety of pedagogical approaches, reflecting on practice, patience and enthusiasm. Teachers can help students retain content in their long-term memory with good recall by including meaningful experiences that engage emotions in daily activities. The use of sustainability education has been shown to increase student performance, promote critical thinking skills and build life skills such as confidence and leadership. The holistic, theme-based approach where students actively engage with content while solving real-world problems is one way to support the long-term retention of ideas. Helping students connect to and understand their place in the world is one of the ultimate goals of education.

Questions to Consider

- ♦ What pedagogical approaches are you currently using in your classroom?
- ♦ Are students interested in and engaged with the content, classroom experiences and communicating with you and others in the classroom?
- ♦ How could you increase the learning that occurs with your students?
- ♦ What skills or training do you feel you need to incorporate problem-based, experiential learning?

References

Barr, S. K., Cross, J. E., & Dunbar, B. H. (2014). *The whole-school sustainability framework: Guiding principles for integrating sustainability into all aspects of a school organization*. https://centerforgreenschools.org/sites/default/files/resource-files/Whole-School_Sustainability_Framework.pdf

Berglund, T., & Gericke, N. (2016). Separated and integrated perspectives on environmental, economic, and social dimensions: An investigation of student views on sustainable development. *Environmental Education Research, 22*(8), 1115–1138.

Birdsall, S. (2010). Empowering students to act: Learning about, through and from the nature of action. *Australian Journal of Environmental Education, 26*, 65–84.

Bodzin, A. (2008). Integrating instructional technologies in a local watershed investigation with urban elementary learners. *Journal of Environmental Education, 39*(2), 47–57.

Borg, C., Gericke, N., Hoglund, H., & Bergman, E. (2012). The barriers encountered by teachers implementing education for sustainable development. *Research in Science & Technological Education, 30*(2), 185–207.

Brandt, R. (1998). *Powerful learning*. Association for Supervision and Curriculum Development.

Burnette, J. L., O'Boyle, E. H., VanEpps, E. M., Pollack, J. M., & Finkel, E. J. (2013). Mind-sets matter: A meta-analytics review of implicit theories and self-regulation. *Psychological Bulletin*, *139*(3), 655–701.

Common Core State Standards (CCSS). (2010). *English language arts standards*. http://www.corestandards.org/ELA-Literacy/.

Coyle, K. J. (2020). Green schools in the United States. In A. Gough & N. Gough (Eds.), *Green schools globally, international explorations in outdoor and environmental education* (pp. 385–401). Springer.

Dale, R. G. (2019). *Influence of the natural setting on environmental education outcomes* [Unpublished master's thesis, Clemson University].

Deans for Impact. (2015). *The science of learning*. Deans for Impact.

Eco-Schools. (2021). *Eco-schools themes*. https://www.ecoschools.global/themes.

Ericsson, K. A., Krampe, R. T., & Tesch-Romer, C. (1993). The role of deliberate practice in the acquisition of expert performance. *Psychological Review*, *100*(3), 363–406.

Farmer, J., Knapp, D., & Benton, G. (2007). An elementary school environmental education field trip: Long-term effects on ecological and environmental knowledge and attitude development. *The Journal of Environmental Education*, *38*(30), 33–42.

Fisman, L. (2005). The effects of a local learning on environmental awareness in children: An empirical investigation. *The Journal of Environmental Education*, *36*(3), 39–50.

Green, C. S., & Dorn, D. S. (1999). The changing classroom: The meaning of shifts in higher education for teaching and learning. In B. A. Pescosolido & R. Aminzade (Eds.), *The social worlds of higher education: Handbook for teaching in a new century* (pp. 59–83). Pine Forge Press.

Hattie, J., & Timperley, H. (2007). The power of feedback. *Review of Educational Research*, *77*(1), 81–112.

Kolb, D. A. (2014). *Experiential learning: Experience as the source of learning and development* (2nd ed.). Pearson Education.

Kotar, M., Guneter, C. E., Metzger, D., & Overholt, J. L. (1998). Curriculum integration: A teacher education model. *Science and Children*, *35*(5), 40–43.

Lieberman, G. A. (2013). *Education and the environment: Creating standards-based programs in schools and districts*. Harvard Education Press.

Louv, R. (2012). *The nature principle: Reconnecting with life in a virtual age*. Algonquin Books.

Maller, C. J. (2009). Promoting children's mental, emotional and social health through contact with nature: A model. *Health Education*, *109*(6), 522–543.

Manni, A., Sporre, K., & Ottander, C. (2013). Mapping what young students understand and value regarding sustainable development. *International Electronic Journal of Environmental Education*, *3*(1), 17–35.

Manolis, C., Burns, D. J., Assudani, R., & Chinta, R. (2013). Assessing experiential learning styles: A methodological reconstruction and validation of the Kolb learning style inventory. *Learning and Individual Differences*, *23*, 44–52.

McDaniel, M. A., Hines, R. J., Waddill, P. J., & Einstein, G. O. (1994). What makes folk tales unique: Content familiarity, causal structure, scripts, or superstructures? *Journal of Experimental Psychology: Learning, Memory, and Cognition*, *20*(1), 169–184.

Moore, M., O'Leary, P., Sinnott, D., & Russell O'Connor, J. (2019). Extending communities of practice: A partnership model for sustainable schools. *Environment Development and Sustainability*, *21*, 1745–1762.

National Council of Teachers of Mathematics. (2000). *Principles and standards*. https://www.nctm.org/standards/.

NGSS. (n.d.). *Quality examples of sciences lessons and units*. https://www. nextgenscience.org/resources/examples-quality-ngss-design.

NGSS Lead States. (2013). *Next generation of science standards: For states, by states*. The National Academies Press.

North American Association for Environmental Education. (2018). *The benefits of environmental education for K–12 students*. https://naaee. org/eepro/research/eeworks/student-outcomes.

North American Association for Environmental Education. (2019). *K–12 environmental education: Guidelines for excellence*. https://naaee. org/eepro/resources/k-12-environmental-education-guidelines.

Omelicheva, M. Y., & Avdeyeva, O. (2008). Teaching with lecture or debate? Testing the effectiveness of traditional versus active learning methods of instruction. *Political Science and Politics*, *41*(3), 603–607.

Pashler, H., McDaniel, M., Rohrer, D., & Bjork, R. (2008). Learning styles: Concepts and evidence. *Psychological Science in the Public Interest*, *9*(3), 105–119.

Pellegrino, J. W., & Hilton, M. L. (2012). *Education for life and work: Developing transferable knowledge and skills in the 21st century.* National Academies Press.

Rainwater, B., & Hartke, J. (2011). *Local leaders in sustainability: Special report from Sundance (A national action plan for greening America's school).* The American Institute of Architects and the U.S. Green Building Council, Inc.

Rosenshine, B., Meister, C., & Chapman, S. (1996). Teaching students to generate questions: A review of the intervention studies. *Review of Educational Research*, *66*(2), 181–221.

Royal Horticulture Society. (2010). *Gardening in schools: A vital tool for children's learning.* National Foundation for Education Research Project.

Ryan, R. M., Weinstein, N., Bernstein, J., Brown, K. W., Mistretta, L., & Gagné, M. (2010). Vitalizing effects of being outdoors and in nature. *Journal of Environmental Psychology*, *30*(2), 159–168.

Shu-Chen, C., Gwo-Jen, H., & Chih-Hung, C. (2019). From reflective observation to active learning: A mobile experiential learning approach for environmental science education. *British Journal of Educational Technology*, *50*(5), 2251–2270.

Smith, G., & Sobel, D. (2010). *Place- and community-based education in schools.* Routledge.

State Education and Environment Roundtable. (2013). *The EIC model.* http://www.seer.org/pages/practices.html.

Sung, H. Y., Hwang, G. J., Wu, P. H., & Lin, D. Q. (2019). Facilitating deep-strategy behaviors and positive learning performances in science inquiry activities with a 3D experiential gaming approach. *Interactive Learning Environments*, *26*(8), 1053–1073.

United Nations Educational, Scientific and Cultural Organization. (2021). *What is education for sustainable development?* https://en.unesco.org/themes/education-sustainable-development/what-is-esd.

Varga, N. L., & Bauer, P. J. (2017). Young adults self-derive and retain new factual knowledge through memory integration. *Memory & Cognition*, *45*, 1014–1027.

Webber, G., & Miller, D. (2016). Progressive pedagogies and teacher education: A review of the literature. *McGill Journal of Education*, *51*(3), 1061–1079.

Wells, N. M. (2000). Effects of greenness on children's cognitive functioning. *Environment and Behavior*, *32*(6), 775–795.

White, R., & Stoeklin, V. L. (2008, October). Nurturing children's biophilia: Developmentally appropriate environmental education for your children. *Collage: Resources for Early Childhood Educators*, 1–11.

Willingham, D. T. (2008). What is developmentally appropriate practice? *American Educator*, 34–39.

Wilson, E. O. (n.d.). https://eowilsonfoundation.org/.

Yeager, D., Walton, G., & Cohen, G. L. (2013). Addressing achievement gaps with psychological interventions. *Phi Delta Kappan*, 62–65.

6

The Management, Aesthetics and Efficiency of a Green School

The environment is where we all meet; where we all have a mutual interest; it is the one thing all of us share.

Lady Bird Johnson (1967)

Vignette

Mr. Atchison and his colleagues had just entered the newly built Hamilton Middle School for an orientation and were truly amazed at what they saw. When you first walked in, there was natural light streaming in as the entire ceiling was glass. If you looked straight ahead, there was a large living wall with ferns, bromeliads, philodendron and pothos. As they walked through the wide hallways, they could see the solar panels on the greenhouse roof at the back of the school. The teachers peeked into one of the classrooms and saw the tall ceilings, large windows that looked out on greenery and upholstered chairs with moveable tables and desks. A couple of the walls were painted in a muted green color, and the entire back wall was white as it could be, written on with erasable pens. There were a lot of cabinets, plenty of

DOI: 10.4324/9781003164524-6

shelf space and an alcove that had a sink. The teachers were delighted that the discussions they had with the architect about what they wanted in the new school had been included in the final design. As they moved on with the orientation, Mr. Atchison smiled to himself and thought, "This is going to be a good year."

Chapter Objectives

♦ Discuss the physical plant, physical health of occupants and aesthetics/environment of a green school.
♦ Highlight various audits that can be conducted on school grounds and what to do with the findings.
♦ Focus on environmental management (waste management and reduction, recycling, composting and air quality and pollution control in a green school).
♦ Describe energy-efficient systems and sustainable practices that can "green" a school campus.

Green School: Plant Management, Physical Health and Improved Performance and Aesthetic/School Environment

As approximately one billion students worldwide (20% of the U.S. population) spend their days in a school, it is important to have a healthy environment that is aesthetically pleasing. The U.S. Environmental Protection Agency (EPA) states that an ideal space for learning would be a green building that preserves the natural environment while creating a healthy space that is environmentally responsible, uses resources efficiently, provides comfort and is durable (2016). With ages ranging between three to 18 years, PreK–12 students have developing brains, lungs and immune systems that are vulnerable to toxins and poor air quality. These same students typically are not asked about where they want to go to school or what is important to them in a school building. They also don't financially support school funding and aren't able to vote for the people who do. So it is crucial for those making decisions to consider how to provide the best environment that supports the learning process. An example of this type of support is the American Rescue Plan, which delivers approximately $130 billion to U.S. PreK–12 schools as part of the Elementary and Secondary School Emergency Relief Fund (ESSER, 2021). These funds were allocated to state and local education agencies and will be used to improve ventilation systems, purchase sanitation supplies, provide professional development to teachers and supply technology for students.

These funds will definitely help PreK–12 schools in becoming more sustainable, though consider the types of decisions that need to be made in relation to a PreK–12 school. For example, what plants will be used in the landscaping? What type of transportation is both efficient and budget-friendly? What curriculum will be either bought or created? And what types of cleaning products will be strong enough to clean but not trigger asthma or respiratory issues? Each school district must make these decisions and many more each time a new PreK–12 building is built or renovated. Incorporating sustainability into these school decisions not only will improve the health and wellness of the people who attend and work in the building but also can be cost-efficient and aesthetically pleasing.

An example of a cost-efficient school is one that has achieved Leadership in Energy and Environmental Design (LEED) certification. This "high-functioning green school will reduce its energy and carbon footprint by 20% or more and reduce its annual utility expenses by $20,000 to $60,000" (Coyle, 2020, p. 398). Water usage will also be reduced, with water usage down as much as 30% and solid waste reduction as high as 90% (Coyle, 2020). This reduction has direct savings for the school district and can reduce stormwater runoff as well. As such, 19 of the top 25 largest U.S. school districts have made a formal commitment to green building, with Washington, DC, Houston, Albuquerque, and Baltimore having built the most LEED certified school buildings (A. Heming, personal communication, August 25, 2021). The U.S. Green Building Council (USGBC) provides third-party verification that a building was designed and constructed using efficiency in water use, energy savings, reduction in greenhouse gas emissions, healthy air quality, use of materials with lower environmental impact and reduced maintenance and operation costs (2019).

There are four types of LEED certification (Platinum, Gold, Silver and Certified), with each level requiring a certain number of points – 80+ points, 60–79 points, 50–59 points and 40–49 points, respectively. Schools can achieve either LEED for Building Design and Construction, referring to the construction or renovation of buildings, or LEED for Operations and Maintenance, referring to the day-to-day operation of existing buildings (USGBC, 2019). Beyond the energy cost savings of building or retrofitting a PreK–12 school to become LEED certified, additional benefits include reduction in health and operating costs, enhanced student learning and an increase in overall school quality (Kats, 2006). In Photo 6.1, the Readington Township Public School District dedicated a large solar panel array in May 2018 that supports energy efficiency within the district. The array is incorporated into the curriculum, with students collecting and analyzing data on energy output.

CREDIT Jonathan Hart, PhD, Readington Township Public School District

Plant Management

An important part of a green school is the actual campus itself. Buildings themselves are an important factor in the learning process as toxins, air quality, acoustics, temperature and exposure to daylight can either help or hinder student performance. Research has shown that "school buildings impact student health and their ability to learn" (Baker & Bernstein, 2012, p. 1). For example, consider the following:

♦ Melatonin cycles in children are disrupted when deprived of natural light, which impacts how alert they are in school (Figueiro & Rea, 2010).

♦ Student performance is impacted (approximately 5–10% decrease) when ventilation standards are not met (Pistochini et al., 2020).

♦ Lead in drinking water "can affect children's cognitive development" (Harvard School of Public Health, 2019, p. 16).

♦ Loud background noise and long reverberation time (the length of time sound lingers in a room) can cause stress and negatively impact students' performance, behavior, speech and learning comprehension (Acoustical Society of America, 2010; Dreger et al., 2015; Klatte et al., 2013).

♦ More than 25% of all American students attend schools considered below standard. In roughly 15,000 schools, the air is "unfit to breathe" (Kats, 2006, p. 8). Bad-quality air can promote asthma attacks that may lead to absenteeism (Sterrett et al., 2014), with "13.8 million missed school days that are attributed to asthma" (U.S. EPA, 2013, para. 2).

♦ The Children's Health Protection Advisory Committee (CHPAC) estimates that "more than 60,000 schools or 46% of U.S. public schools have environmental conditions that contribute to poor indoor environmental quality, including allergens from cockroaches, rodents, dust mites and fungi, as well as respiratory irritants from sources of formaldehyde, volatile organic compounds and nitrogen dioxide" (2011, p. 1).

- Teachers report the "highest percentage of work-related asthma cases in the U.S., compared to other non-industrial occupations" (Angelon-Gaetz et al., 2016, p. 730).
- Dust, mold and certain types of chemicals (e.g., flame retardant, phthalates and stain-repellent chemicals) can cause concentration problems, headaches and dizziness (Kim et al., 2007).
- "Approximately 15% of schools had lead levels in drinking water that exceeded the EPA's drinking water standard" (Karliner, 2005, p. 17). Lead is found in soil, paint and drinking water, and children absorb 50% of the lead they are exposed to.

Taking into account these health issues, a school should provide quiet classrooms that have appropriate natural sunlight and quality indoor air circulation, use healthy products, and create outdoor spaces that promote physical activity and connect to the curriculum. Along with these items, a green school building should conserve energy and water, incorporate sustainable building materials (e.g., reclaimed wood or steel, recycled plastic or precast concrete slabs), consider the outdoors during building design (e.g., space for food gardens and a compost area) and incorporate the natural environment (Center for Green Schools, 2018). Considering all of these aspects, a school building manager has an incredibly important role to play in supporting and furthering a high-quality learning environment. In Photo 6.2, a student at the Colegio Santa Francisca Romana school is actively engaged within the maker space.

Along with the importance of a school plant manager, there are numerous reasons that school districts are hiring coordinators to oversee environment-focused efforts. Motivations for hiring include being a "champion" for sustainability and complying to city or state policy or personal advocacy (Gutierrez & Metzger, 2015). Much of what these coordinators focus on is implementing new policies, documenting sustainability metrics such as energy use or waste diversion or developing sustainability-related district

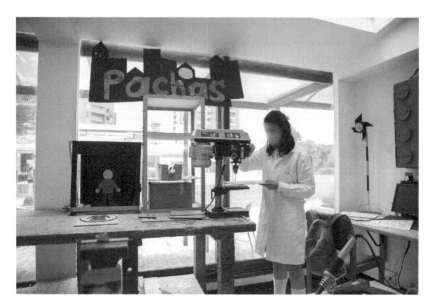

CREDIT Kattia Marcela Lozada Mariño, Colegio Santa Francisca Romana

policy (Gutierrez & Metzger, 2015). These staff members may or may not be directly in charge of implementing sustainability initiatives, which means that a plant manager at an individual school is likely not someone who has a background in environmental management. This means that a school plant manager will need training in how to work with new systems, especially replacing filters more often (Barr et al., 2013).

Physical Health and Improved Performance

When considering physical health, comfort greatly impacts how we feel and relate to the world. Physical comfort encompasses the appropriate amount of "light, sound, temperature, air quality and 'links to nature'" (Barrett et al., 2015, p. 119). For quality student learning, it is important that teachers and students feel comfortable during the school day. When schools are built or renovated, much of the design and discussion of the school layout is completed without teacher or student input, though they are the ones that spend 25–40 hours per week in these physical structures. It is possible to provide a sense of ownership (personalization of a room) and flexibility (meets the needs of individuals) in classroom design, with teachers and students showing interest in the following items:

♦ Having the ability to arrange student seating in interactive and non-interactive arrangements, including a reading or IT space if room is available (Ramli et al., 2015).
♦ Including variation of textures, colors and materials on walls and ceilings – when the classroom space is intimate and personalized, students are more involved in the learning process (Ulrich, 2004).
♦ Variation in the types of classroom furniture, including flexible seating (soft and upholstered chairs) and moveable tables or desks, as a unique, student-centered room can positively impact behavior and learning (Leung & Fung, 2005).
♦ Exposure to daylight, rather than artificial light, as natural daylight has been shown to support up to a 20% increase in math and reading performance with students (Tanner, 2009).
♦ Views of the natural outdoors or gardens – there is a weak correlation of outdoor views with an increase in learning (Barrett et al., 2015).

Additional studies have been conducted that further show student learning performance is impacted by the surrounding environment. A review of 1,500 studies completed by Carnegie Mellon University's Building Investment Decision Support (BIDS) program focused on both worker and student performance in sustainably designed buildings (2005).

The tasks done by "knowledge workers" (including non-factory white collar workers) – such as reading comprehension, synthesis of information, writing, calculations and communications are very similar to the work students do. Large-scale studies correlating green or high performance features with increased productivity and performance in many non-academic institutions are therefore relevant to schools. (Kats, 2006, p. 9)

These studies found the following:

- Improvement in health issues such as asthma, headaches and respiratory problems can be achieved through good air circulation and appropriate filtration systems (Carnegie Mellon, 2005).
- Concentrations of carbon dioxide (CO_2) "are among the dominant pollutants in classrooms due to the density of occupation" and negatively affect cognitive functioning (Wargocki & Wyon, 2012, p. 587. Hence, including CO_2 sensors in classrooms should be considered.
- Teaching quality and student achievement are higher when teachers are able to control the temperature (Schneider, 2002).
- Classroom acoustics can be optimized through the use of "high-quality acoustical ceiling tiles, lined ductwork and heating and cooling systems with appropriately placed vents designed to lower background noise in the classroom" (Center for Green Schools, 2018, para. 5).
- Increased natural light, without glare, increases test scores, decreases behavior issues and helps to promote higher student achievement (Lemasters, 1997). Installing sunblinds that can be manipulated by the teachers would alleviate increased room temperature.
- All schools (including green schools and LEED-certified or traditional schools) need to consider occupant well-being as even the best-designed buildings should monitor occupant comfort throughout the school year (Al horr et al., 2016).

A further review of research studies found a positive relationship between the school building condition and student achievement (Hewitt, 2017).

Students attending school in buildings that are assessed as being in poor condition do not perform as well as students in school buildings assessed as being in good condition. The amount of difference ranges from 3 percent to 10 percent. This is a very astonishingly high ratio of difference when considering things like achievement scores. (Earthman, 2018, p. 58)

As these students will likely attend these same schools over several years, this "discrepancy in achievement scores could well be multiplied many times" (Earthman, 2018, p. 58). These findings don't directly focus on green schools, though the assumption is that if a school has been built or renovated to LEED specifications, it would be considered a building in good condition. Ultimately, conditions for optimum student learning include a classroom with few distractions, natural or indirect lighting, low ambient sounds, colorful, stimulating walls that aren't cluttered, teacher-controlled thermostat, high-quality chairs and desks/tables and efficient air circulation (Barrett et al., 2015).

Another important factor that impacts student performance, though not often discussed, is teacher morale. The teaching profession has a fairly stressful work regimen, and adding poor building conditions can distract or negatively impact how they approach teaching (Kerlin et al., 2015). The effects of poor working conditions include increased teacher absenteeism, less effort put into teaching and low job satisfaction (Earthman & Lemasters, 2009). As highlighted previously, green schools have shown improvements in health conditions, reduced absenteeism, had higher teacher retention (Kats, 2006) and an increase in student test scores and performance (Filardo, 2021).

Aesthetic/School Environment

The "look and feel" of a building speaks volumes as to the care and concern of those responsible for the school facilities. Well-kept landscape, natural light effused in the hallways and fresh air help to create a quality environment for those who work and attend school. In comparison, a weed-strewn front entrance, broken fixtures and peeling paint can create an unwelcoming environment that impacts health and causes discontent for teachers, staff and students. The aesthetic or visual appeal of a building can convey a feeling of comfort or discomfort depending upon how well cared for or dilapidated it is. Children are sensitive to their surroundings "because, as a part of their development, they actively look for cues on how to behave, who they are, or what they can accomplish" (Durán-Narucki, 2008, p. 284). So a school building that shows signs of deterioration may convey to students, parents, teachers and staff that, like the building, they have been forgotten.

Typically, school buildings in poor condition are where lower-income students of color are more likely to be. These students are "30% to 50% more likely to have respiratory issues such as asthma and allergies that lead to increased absenteeism, and diminished learning and test scores" (Filardo, 2016, p. 19), which raises a social justice question. Fixing a deteriorating building can actually improve student education, which is a simple way to ameliorate the issue. Using LEED certification and other green school aspects such as outdoor classrooms, gardens and farm-to-table cafeteria and using the building as a learning tool will also help to show students, teachers and staff that they matter. For example, Ohio leads the nation with more than 560 total schools and childcare centers being LEED certified (Etienne, 2020). Specifically, Cincinnati Public Schools (a mostly urban district) and South-Western City Schools have close to 40% of their schools certified. California, Pennsylvania, Illinois, Maryland and Florida are the other top states that have emphasized LEED school certification (Heming, 2017). As well, teachers and staff from over 180 school districts, including 19 of the top 25 largest districts,

> receive dedicated training and support at no cost from the Center for Green Schools. The support they receive includes monthly virtual education; an annual in-person summit; and an application-based, year-long fellowship program. These districts collectively serve over 8 million students. (A. Zusman, personal communication, September 22, 2021)

This type of dedication from school districts, teachers and staff will positively impact millions of students while creating an environment that promotes energy efficiency, water conservation and environmental project-based learning.

Environmental School Audits

One of the many positive aspects of a green school is that it can become a hands-on educational opportunity for students. If a school has solar panels, students can use an application to view the ebbs and flows of energy production. They can also conduct water, energy and waste audits to better understand how the school is doing with efficiency. The World Wildlife Federation has high-quality audits for energy, water, transportation, schoolyard habitats, healthy living, etc. (2021).

Most of the audits are broken down by grade level bands (K–2, 3–5, 6–8, and 9–12) and include lesson plans, baseline and post-action audits (see chapter references for a link to the WWF audit website). Depending on the type of audit completed, enlisting the help of the school plant manager (energy, water, healthy schools and consumption and waste), physical education teacher (healthy living), cafeteria staff (sustainable foods), administration (transportation) or other experts would be crucial if actions are to be taken.

In relation to an energy audit, students could do an assessment of the physical structure of the building and other facilities (e.g., HVAC system), natural and artificial lighting, operations, classroom temperature, etc. Green Schools Alliance has partnered with Noveda Technologies to provide management tools to member schools so that real-time consumption data can be tracked (2021). This monitoring of data could help students (and staff) better understand sources of waste and optimize consumption. Having administrative permission and including the school plant manager would be vital for the success of this audit.

A focus on the school cafeteria and sustainable foods could include an analysis of what is being eaten versus thrown away, types of cutlery and plates being used, what is recyclable or compostable and the nutrition value of food being served. An audit of the overall cafeteria could include how lunch menus are distributed (paper vs. paperless), what happens to leftover food and whether there is a "share table" and connection to local farms for food products. Again, including the cafeteria staff in the audit will ease the process of achieving actionable items.

To better understand the health of school-building occupants, physical-exercise audits can be conducted. As childhood obesity is a significant precursor to adult obesity, incorporating physical exercise and good eating habits early in life is important (Jones et al., 2013). For example, the Green Schools Travel (GST) program in Ireland has increased the number of students walking and biking to school (2019) and provides a tool kit with resources to help teachers and schools with reducing car and bus trips, keeping statistics on walkers and bikers and numerous problem-based projects the students can conduct.

Energy-Efficient Systems and Sustainable Practices

Of the 130,930 PreK–12 schools in the U.S. (National Center for Education Statistics, 2018), approximately half need "to update or replace multiple systems like heating, ventilation, and air conditioning (HVAC) or plumbing" (U.S. Government Accounting Office, 2020, para. 1). More than one-third of PreK–12 public schools have portable buildings, with 45% in either fair or poor condition (Congressional Research Service, 2020). U.S. schools are the second largest sector of public infrastructure spending, though funding for schools was down 31% in 2017 compared to 2008 (Center on Budget and Policy Priorities, 2018). Approximately $49 billion is spent annually on PreK–12 building infrastructure, though it is estimated that the U.S. should be spending $145 billion per year (a deficit of $96 billion) to maintain, operate and renew facilities (Filardo, 2021; USGBC, 2016). Consequently, more funding is needed to support high-quality school facilities.

HVAC systems are a necessity for schools to heat and cool buildings. There are specific types of HVAC technologies that are more energy efficient, meet the EPA's Energy Star rating, are widely available, use repurposed materials, are eligible for energy-saving tax credits and/or reduce energy costs by 20% to 30%. For example, a geothermal heat pump uses the Earth's energy to pump warm air from the ground during the winter and draws the hot air out and back into the ground in the summer. The pump does not rely on fossil fuels and does not emit carbon dioxide. When replacing an entire HVAC system is not feasible, certain smart thermostats, as discussed in Chapter 4, can allow plant managers to pre-program HVAC systems which can cut down on energy use. Retrofitting an HVAC system can have the added benefit of increasing fresh air in classrooms to prevent contagious viruses such as COVID-19 from spreading.

In April 2021, the American Society of Heating and Air-Conditioning Engineers (ASHAE) and the Center for Green Schools published the first known report on air quality in schools during the COVID-19 outbreak. In a request for how schools were "implementing protective measures to improve indoor air quality (IAQ), prioritizing ventilation and filtration to reduce the transmission of the virus" (Center for Green Schools, 2021, para. 3), over 4,000 school in 24 states responded to the survey. One of the main issues that schools reported is that the schools are not designed to implement the recommended strategies. Schools have been able to upgrade filters and many are monitoring IAQ, though cost constraints and old building infrastructure are still a challenge. Some of the recommended IAQ strategies include the following:

- ◆ Increase fresh air through mechanical ventilation.
  - Increase outdoor air supply through the building's heating, ventilation, and air conditioning (HVAC) system.
  - Implement a flushing process between occupancy periods where the HVAC system runs for a pre-specified duration or until a target of clean air changes has been reached.
- ◆ Increase outdoor air through the use of operable windows.
  - Open windows to increase the outdoor flow.
  - Place fans in windows to exhaust room air to the outdoors.

◆ Remove airborne contaminants through filtration.
  • Upgrade to filters with higher minimum efficiency reporting values (MERV) ratings, with MERV 13 or better as a target for removing airborne viral particles in recirculating systems (MERV ratings range from 1–16, with 16 being the more efficient filtration).
  • Install air cleaners with high-efficiency particulate air (HEPA) filters (HEPA filters are no less than 99.7% efficient at capturing human-generated viral particles) (Hoang & Heming, 2021, p. 2).

Additional investment, as part of the American Rescue Plan, should allow schools to be able to invest in updating building infrastructure to better manage COVID-19 and future air-quality issues.

As part of this retrofitting, schools should consider renewable energy sources that are sustainable, don't run out or are endless, such as the sun. Environmentally sustainable energy systems include solar energy, wind turbines and biomass. There are others such as hydro or tidal energy, though these may not be feasible for many school districts. Vegetative roofing, also called living or green roofs, can help to control water runoff, acts as a barrier to outside temperatures, increases the life of the roof membrane, improves air quality and can be aesthetically pleasing (Koroxenidis & Theodosiou, 2021). Rainwater harvesting is another way to conserve resources and is essentially the collection of rainfall from the surfaces on or surrounding the school building. Incorporating a 10-kiloliter or 2,641-gallon rainwater tank for a school with a 200–1,000 student population could be used for flushing toilets or irrigation purposes. Other ways to promote conservation is to include native landscaping, install low-flow fixtures (faucets, showers, toilets and urinals), use low-emitting materials (adhesives, paints and carpeting) and recycle (paper, plastic and glass) (Gordon, 2010).

A daylighting system is useful in a green school as it increases natural lighting and has a lighting control system that is daylight responsive (Costanzo et al., 2017). When ambient lighting is provided from daylight, electric lighting automatically reduces.

This system is designed so that windows and skylights are placed to avoid direct sun on desks and tables as well as into students' eyes. When building or renovating a school, it is best to incorporate daylighting into the design so that building orientation (majority of spaces facing south), climate and lighting can be optimized (Leslie, 2004). The goal is to reduce installed lighting in the school building, especially classrooms. Incorporating dimmable lighting and photosensor controls will help to maximize visual comfort.

Development of Environmental Management That Supports Sustainability

As of 2021, there were 2,607 LEED certified PreK–12 schools, with another 2,219 that are currently registered to achieve LEED certification (A. Heming, personal communication, September 1, 2021). These buildings will have a reduced impact on the environment, and the inhabitants will enjoy enhanced health and higher productivity. These green schools are built with sustainable or recycled materials, incorporate rainwater collection systems using green roofs or rain tanks and create water-efficient landscapes. Though these schools are a small fraction of the overall number of PreK–12 schools in the world, they are growing quickly. If all 130,930 PreK–12 U.S. public schools used 100% clean energy, "it would be the equivalent of taking one in 7 cars off the road or retiring 18 coal plants" (Sierra Club, 2021, para. 3).

The USGBC (2021) has highlighted general characteristics that help give a good understanding of what can be done to create a green school (some of which have already been discussed in this chapter). The characteristics are as follows:

- ◆ Maximum energy savings (conserves energy and natural resources).
- ◆ Efficient use of water (conserve fresh drinking water and helps manage stormwater runoff.
- ◆ Decreases the burden on municipal water and wastewater treatment.

♦ Encourages waste-management efforts to benefit the local community and region.

♦ Reduces greenhouse gas emissions.

♦ Includes healthier indoor-air quality.

♦ Increases use of recycled materials.

♦ Optimizes use of resources and sensitivity to their impacts.

♦ Reduces maintenance and operation costs.

♦ Removes toxic materials from places where children learn and play.

♦ Employs daylighting strategies and improves classroom acoustics.

♦ Encourages recycling.

♦ Promotes habitat protection.

♦ Reduces demand on local landfills.

Purchasing materials and products from local businesses puts money into the community while also developing the local economy. If a school is being constructed or renovated, the facility planners can research local contractors who may specialize in the use of sustainable materials and construction.

Conclusions

The majority of school buildings in the world are not built as aesthetically pleasing spaces and do not consider student or teacher voices in the construction of these buildings. The ideal space for learning includes efficient systems, provides comfort, includes natural light, quiet indoor and outdoor spaces for learning and is aesthetically-pleasing. A number of schools have incorporated some of these ideas through LEED certification, which promotes energy and water efficiency as well as decreases a school's carbon footprint. As school buildings can impact student health and the ability to learn, it is important to consider the amount of natural light, noise level, air quality, allergen exposure and lead levels in drinking water. There is an equity issue as students of color are more likely to be in buildings that are in poor condition. As current funding on PreK–12 building infrastructure is far below what is needed, part of the American Rescue Plan funds should be used on blighted schools. Once a school building has incorporated green initiatives or has LEED certification, it can become a way for students to learn about systems, consumption, waste, healthy living, transportation, etc. Conducting different types of audits will help better understand how things work in the school building.

Questions to Consider

- ◆ Look around your school. Do you feel it is aesthetically pleasing as you drive up to the entrance, walk down halls or peer into the bathrooms?
- ◆ What are ways that the building could be made more aesthetically pleasing, include more efficient systems or develop quiet spaces for learning?
- ◆ Consider the type of audits you might carry out with students. What might positively impact changes?
- ◆ Is the school plant manager, cafeteria staff or administration open to making system changes? Consider opening a dialogue with administration as a starting place.

References

Acoustical Society of America. (2010). *American national standard acoustical performance criteria, design requirements, and guidelines for schools, part 1: Permanent schools*. Success for Kids with Hearing Loss.

Al horr, Y., Arif, M., Katafygiotou, M., Mazroei, A., Kaushik, A., & Elsarrag, E. (2016). Impact of indoor environmental quality on occupant well-being and comfort: A review of the literature. *International Journal of Sustainable Built Environment*, *5*, 1–11.

Angelon-Gaetz, K., Richardson, D. B., Marshall, S. W., & Hernandez, M. L. (2016). Exploration of the effects of classroom humidity levels on teachers' respiratory symptoms. *International Archives of Occupational and Environmental Health*, *89*(5), 729–737.

Baker, L., & Bernstein, H. (2012). *The impact of school buildings on student health and performance.* www.centerforgreenschools.org/green-schools-are-better-learning

Barr, S., Dunbar, B., & Cross, J. (2013). *Linking performance and experience: An analysis of green schools. Institute for the built environment.* www.dlrgroup.com/media/424339/Linking_Performance_Experience_CSU-Research.pdf

Barrett, P., Davies, F., Zhang, Y., & Barrett, L. (2015). The impact of classroom design on pupils' learning: Final results of a holistic, multi-level analysis. *Building and Environment, 89,* 118–133.

Carnegie Mellon University (BIDS). (2005). *Building investment decisions support.* BIDS Report.

Center for Green Schools. (2018). *Green school buildings are better for teachers and students.* www.centerforgreenschools.org/green-schools-are-better-learning

Center for Green Schools. (2021). *IAQ in schools report.* Indoor Air Quality.

Center on Budget and Policy Priorities. (2018). *School infrastructure needs a funding infusion.* www.cbpp.org/blog/school-infrastructure-needs-a-funding-infusion

Children's Health Protection Advisory Committee. (2011). *Report of the indoor environment workgroup on indoor environment.* Indoor Environment Study.

Congressional Research Service. (2020). *School construction and renovation.* CRS Reports

Costanzo, V., Evola, G., & Marletta, L. (2017). A review of daylighting strategies in schools: State of the art and expected future trends. *Buildings, 41*(7), (1–21).

Coyle, K. J. (2020). Green schools in the United States. In A. Gough & N. Gough (Eds.), *Green schools globally, international explorations in Outdoor and environmental education* (pp. 385–401). Springer.

Dreger, S., Meyer, N., Fromme, H., & Bolte, G. (2015). Environmental noise and incident mental health problems: A prospective cohort study among school children in Germany. *Environmental Research, 143,* 49–54.

Durán-Narucki, V. (2008). School building condition, school attendance, and academic achievement in New York City public schools:

A mediation model. *Journal of Environmental Psychology*, *28*, 278–286.

Earthman, G. I. (2018). Examining methodological differences: Research on the relationship between school building condition and student achievement. *Educational Planning*, *25*(3), 47–61.

Earthman, G. I., & Lemasters, L. K. (2009). Teacher attitudes about classroom conditions. *Journal of Educational Administration*, *47*(3), 323–335.

ESSER. (2021). *Elementary and secondary school emergency relief fund*. ESSER Fund.

Etienne, M. (2020). *Ohio's list of LEED-certified schools highlights the state's dedication to making a global impact*. Global Leader.

Figueiro, M., & Rea, M. S. (2010). Lack of short-wavelength light during the school day delays dim light melatonin onset (DLMO) in middle school students. *Neuroendocrinology Letters*, *31*(1).

Filardo, M. (2016). *State of our schools: America's K–12 facilities 2021*. 21st Century School Fund.

Filardo, M. (2021). *State of our schools: America's K–12 facilities 2021*. 21st Century School Fund.

Gordon, D. (2010). *Green schools as high performance learning facilities*. National Clearinghouse for Education Facilities.

Green Schools Alliance. (2021). *Utility dashboard*. www.greenschoolsalliance.org/service/utilitydashboard

Green Schools Travel Program. (2019). *Toolkit for school travel*. School Travel Toolkit.

Gutierrez, D., & Metzger, A. B. (2015). *Managing sustainability in school districts: A profile of sustainability staff in the K–12 sector*. Center for Green Schools Research Article.

Harvard School of Public Health. (2019). *Foundations for student success: How school buildings influence student health, thinking and performance*. Schools for Health.

Heming, A. (2017). *Number of LEED-certified schools hits 2,000*. LEED-Certified Schools.

Hewitt, C. D. (2017). *An analytic synthesis of research studies dealing with the relationship between school building condition and student academic achievement* (Doctoral dissertation). Virginia Polytechnic and State University. ProQuest Dissertations Publishing. https://vtechworks.lib.vt.edu/handle/10919/89606

Hoang, A., & Heming, A. (2021). *How schools implemented air quality measures to protect occupants from COVID-19*. Air Quality Measures to Protect Against COVID-19.

Johnson, C. A. (1967). *Lady bird Johnson*. www.ladybirdjohnson.org/

Jones, R. A., Hinkley, T., Okely, A. D., & Salmon, J. (2013). Tracking physical activity and sedentary behavior in childhood: A systematic review. *American Journal of Preventive Medicine, 44*(6), 651–658.

Karliner, J. (2005). *The little green schoolhouse: Thinking big about ecological sustainability, children's environmental health and K–12 education in the U.S.A.* The Green Schools Initiative.

Kats, G. (2006). *Greening America's schools: Cost and benefits. A capital E report*. www.usgbc.org/resources/greening-america039s-schools-costs-and-benefits

Kerlin, S., Santos, R., & Bennett, W. (2015). Green schools as learning laboratories? Teachers' perceptions of their first year in a new green middle school. *Journal of Sustainability Education, 8*. Green Middle School.

Kim, J. L., Elfman, L., Mi, Y., Wieslander, G., Smedje, G., & Norback, D. (2007). Indoor molds, bacteria, microbial volatile organic compounds and plasticizers in schools: Associations with asthma and respiratory symptoms in pupils. *Indoor Air, 17*(2), 153–163.

Klatte, M., Bergstrom, K., & Lachmann, T. (2013). Does noise affect learning? A short review on noise effects on cognitive performance in children. *Frontiers in Psychology, 4*, article 578. Cognitive Performance.

Koroxenidis, E., & Theodosiou, T. (2021). Comparative environmental and economic evaluation of green roofs under Mediterranean climate conditions: Extensive green roofs a potentially preferable solution. *Journal of Cleaner Production, 311*, 1–17.

Lemasters, L. K. (1997). *A synthesis of studies pertaining to facilities, student achievement, and student behavior* (Publication No. 9722616) (Doctoral dissertation). Virginia Polytechnic and State University. ProQuest Dissertations Publishing.

Leslie, R. P. (2004). *Guide for daylighting schools*. Lighting Research Center.

Leung, M., & Fung, I. (2005). Enhancement of classroom facilities of primary schools and its impact on learning behaviors of students. *Facilities*, *23*(13), 585–594.

National Center for Education Statistics. (2018). *Educational institutions*. https://nces.ed.gov/fastfacts/display.asp?id=84

Pistochini, T., Caton, M., Modera, M., Outcault, S., Sanguinetti, A., Rengie Chan, W., Dutton, S., Singer, B., & Li, W. (2020). *Improving ventilation and indoor environmental quality in California K–12 schools*. California Energy Commission. www.energy.ca.gov/publications/2020/improving-ventilation-and-indoor-environmental-quality-california-schools

Ramli, N. H., Ahmad, S., & Masri, M. H. (2015). Improving the classroom physical environment: Classroom users' perception. *Social and Behavioral Sciences*, *101*, 221–119.

Schneider, M. (2002). *Do school facilities affect academic outcomes? National clearinghouse for education facilities*. https://eric.ed.gov/?id=ED470979

Sierra Club. (2021). *100% clean energy school districts*. www.sierraclub.org/climate-parents/100-clean-energy-school-districts

Sterrett, W. L., Imig, S., & Moore, D. (2014). U.S. Department of education green ribbon schools: Leadership insights and implications. *Journal of Organizational Learning and Leadership*, *12*(2), 1–18.

Tanner, C. K. (2009). Effects of school design on student outcomes. *Journal of Educational Administration*, *47*(3), 381–400.

Ulrich, C. (2004). A place of their own: Children and the physical environment. *Human Ecology*, *32*(2), 11–14.

U.S. EPA. (2013). *Managing asthma in the school environment*. www.epa.gov/iaq-schools/managing-asthma-school-environment.

U.S. EPA (2016). *Green building*. https://archive.epa.gov/greenbuilding/web/html/about.html.

U.S. Government Accounting Office. (2020). *K–12 education: School districts frequently identified multiple building systems needing updates or replacement*. www.gao.gov/products/gao-20-494

U.S. Green Building Council. (2016). *Advancing green schools*. http://centerforgreenschools.org/

U.S. Green Building Council. (2019). *LEED-certified schools*. www.usgbc.org/articles/explore-30-leedcertified-schools-2019

U.S. Green Building Council. (2021). *The four pillars of green building at USGBC*. www.usgbc.org/articles/four-pillars-green-building-usgbc.

Wargocki, P., & Wyon, D. P. (2012). Providing better thermal and air quality conditions in school classrooms would be cost-effective. *Building and Environment, 59*, 581–589.

World Wildlife Federation. (2021). *Environmental audits for K–2, 3–5, 6–8, and 9–12*. www.nwf.org/Eco-Schools-USA/Pathways/Audit.

7

Policy, Safety and Diversity, Equity and Inclusion Within a Green School

"You cannot get through a single day without having an impact on the world around you.
What you do makes a difference and you have to decide what kind of a difference you want to make."

Jane Goodall

Vignette

Eastern High School was in a rural school district, close to the Appalachian Mountains. The principal, Mrs. Haeckl, had wanted to include the local environment more in both the school curriculum and the service-learning projects completed each year. She had finally set up a meeting with the Alliance for Appalachia group to get a better sense of non-profits who could support Eastern High School (https://theallianceforappalachia.org/where-we-work/). Mrs. Haeckl was interested in having the students better understand where they were from, a biologically diverse area surrounded by majestic mountains. She also felt that the students would appreciate their community more if they were involved in experiential

DOI: 10.4324/9781003164524-7

learning experiences. As the Appalachian Trail ran fairly close to the school, Mrs. Haeckl was thinking that the students could learn about trail stewardship by taking care of the local greenway. She thought consulting with a non-profit group could provide leadership in the next steps. As the meeting was concluding, Mrs. Haeckl felt that she now had the information needed to share at the next faculty meeting and was excited about the next steps.

Chapter Objectives

♦ Share an overview of policy that focuses on creating and maintaining green schools.
♦ Describe non-profit organizations and how they support school districts with sustainability practices.
♦ Highlight safety considerations in how students interact and use tools, including supervision guidelines.
♦ Discuss diversity, equity and inclusion in relation to green schools and sustainability and what can be done to mitigate some of the issues.

Government, Policy, Non-profits and Green Schools

Government and Policy

The policies established at local, state and national levels impact K–12 schools and consequently play a crucial role in incentivizing school districts to create green schools. As much of the K–12 school-building infrastructure in the U.S. (and in many other countries) was designed and built over four decades ago, an acceleration of state and national policies is needed so that schools can be either updated or torn down to put up new buildings. School districts, local officials and individual communities can also play an important role in encouraging renovation of schools.

Though improving school infrastructure is an important concern with regard to PreK–12 schools, during the COVID-19 pandemic, schools have been grappling with policy on how to safely bring students back into the classroom. Lower-income students and people of color have been disproportionately impacted by the virus. One of the ways that some PreK–12 schools have been altering their understanding of space is using the outdoors more in their teaching. Establishing "outdoor learning policies should be rooted in environmental justice and equity" (Green Schoolyards America, para. 2). Policy and funding that reflects equitable distribution of funds can ensure that all students have quality resources to help them thrive. The use of outdoor space is being promoted by the National COVID-19 Outdoor Learning Initiative. The goal of the Green Schoolyards America COVID-19 initiative is to use the outdoors as a learning tool that is also cost-effective, increases school space capacity and includes access to fresh air (2021).

This type of equity initiative has been supported by the local government. In 2008, the U.S. Conference of Mayors passed a resolution that would promote green infrastructure, sustainable purchasing programs and new green school construction (Rainwater, 2011). School districts operate independently of local government, though mayors, city council members and city managers can influence schools through planning and

Readington Middle School (RMS) Whitehouse Station, New Jersey Using the Outdoors

Typically, schools use the outdoors for sports, with practice fields taking up large amounts of space. At RMS, they include competitive sports, though they also participate in the USDA's Healthier U.S. School Challenge. which promotes good nutrition and physical activity. Students also participate in Project Adventure, which is an adventure-based, experiential curriculum, and other outdoor cooperative team-building activities. Each grade emphasizes some type of outdoor activity, with sixth grade conducting nature outings at a local farm, seventh grade participating in a "Walk in the Woods," which is led by local guides and focuses on signs of human impact and how to promote sustainable farming practices, and eighth grade pilot outdoor vertical gardens. At RMS, the students are also building an outdoor environmental monitoring station to collect, analyze and share weather and climate information over time.

zoning and encourage school districts to design energy-efficient, high-performance school buildings. As well, state legislators can set green building standards, encourage policies on school operations and maintenance and provide financing opportunities (USGBC, 2010). In 2010, the U.S. Green Building Council (USGBC) held a State Legislative Summit and published a guide for state legislators on best policy practices for greening schools. Numerous state legislators were involved in the summit and supported LEED certification for newly built schools.

As the Tenth Amendment gives individual states decision-making power over education, standards and policies can differ from one state to the next. Each state has a board of education that oversees curriculum, teaching methods, instructional materials, enrollment and graduation requirements, school-building maintenance, renovation and construction. The budget for these items comes from the state (approximately 48%), with local resources contributing approximately 44% (mainly property taxes) and the last 8% comes from the federal government. School districts with a higher socioeconomic base will have more resources, so the quality of education varies from state to state, city to city and even district to district. This inequality factors into the quality of school buildings and teachers and student-to-teacher ratio. All of this information points to the main issue of inequality as some school districts are able to provide high-quality green schools with good air-filtration systems, and other districts lack the resources to even repair old HVAC systems.

School districts, including superintendents and school boards, have wide latitude in creating and implementing environmental policies. For example, the Newport School in Bucaramanga, Colombia, is part of a network of nine schools that focus on three platforms: human centeredness, high academic performance and global connections. The emphasis is on healthy living and being active citizens, which is conducted through project learning. School districts can adopt a green school resolution, which can focus on using only sustainable cleaning materials, advancing green-school-only construction and leveraging utility cost savings from energy-efficient systems to fund future green building retrofits. A project-based curriculum that emphasizes sustainability shouldn't cost too much and could be developed by a school district-wide committee that uses existing resources to incorporate environmental projects into a grade-level curriculum.

This type of committee would need the support and guidance of teachers who, when it comes to influencing K–12 educational policy, are a largely overlooked group. Due to lack of time, the inability to leave the classroom and little to no training in policy development, teachers rarely engage in policy and advocacy. Data support these conclusions as 70% of teachers believe they have no input in district decision-making (Duffett et al., 2008). In 2015, the National Network of State Teachers of the Year wrote a white paper that highlights ways to involve K–12 teachers in the policy process. The report recommends that teachers receive training in becoming leaders and understanding how educational policy is created and influenced by others. Other recommendations include that every state legislature have an educator advisory council and fellowships be developed so that educators work with federal and state legislatures on K–12 education policy development.

If teachers are interested in pursuing this type of activism, there are

Newport School, Bucaramanga, Colombia
Colegio Santa Francesca Romana, Bogota, Colombia
Advocacy for the Environment

Newport School is part of Redcol, the leading educational network in Colombia with a focus on global connections, project-based learning and being an active citizen. Teachers work with the other schools in the network to establish curriculum. They also collect data and share information with the community as well as other schools. There is frequent teacher training that permeates every decision. Colegio Santa Francisca Romana – "Pachas" is also part of the Redcol network; the school community works with a focus on grassroots support of the local biodiversity. The sustainability leader has great latitude to incorporate sustainability into the school curriculum. She has been able to accomplish a great deal with the support of the administration. The whole school community is committed to contributing to the SDGs, or Sustainability Development Goals.

numerous organizations that provide teachers training in how to work with policy makers, advocate for specific policy and share their ideas with others (see resource list at the end of the book for organization information). In relation to green schools, advocating for energy efficiency and promoting sustainability, teachers that spend 50% of their time on sustainability-related work can apply for a fellowship through the Center for Green Schools through the School Sustainability Leaders Network (2018). At Colegio Los Nogales, the sustainability coordinator has previous educational policy experience that helps him focus on important yearly goals (Photo 7.1).

Impact of Non-profits

One way that school districts can better use the funds given to them is to leverage their purchasing power. Some non-profit organizations have developed grassroots initiatives that support sustainability practices. For example, the Green Schools Alliance (GSA) is a collaborative for public school districts that work together to leverage their purchasing power to support "sustainable alternatives and promote market transformation, and influence national policy decisions" (2021, para. 1). The collaborative involves 27 U.S. school districts, with nine of the largest school

CREDIT Pedro Felipe Linares, Colegio Los Nogales

districts, including New York City Department of Education, Chicago Public Schools, Gwinnett County Public Schools, Houston Independent School District and San Diego Unified School District. GSA works with small, medium and large school districts to promote sustainable product purchases and save an average 20% through those purchases. They also help schools lower energy costs by using a utility dashboard that allows energy monitoring or more cutting-edge technology that helps with conservation measures as well as educate students on energy management.

There are numerous other non-profit organizations ready to help school districts, teachers and community members from influencing policy makers to curriculum development (see resource list for further information). The more that school districts are able to work together, the more likely they are to influence policy and policy makers. For example, the Center for Green Schools has a coordinator that works with over 300 school districts across the U.S. that resource share and network (P. Beierle, personal communication, March 25, 2021). Typically, these are medium to large school districts that have a sustainability manager. School districts that are interested in renewable energy can create clean energy resolutions that not only impact their own schools but also support local businesses and the communities that are influenced by these decisions. The U.S. Department of Energy's Better Building Solution Center has a

Hamilton Southeastern School Corporation (HSE), Fishers, Indiana Working With Organizations

It does take time to establish a relationship with outside organizations, though it's worth it if each group gets something from the collaboration. HSE has partnered with numerous organizations to benefit students. For example, HSE's food services has partnered with the parent-teacher organization and the local food bank to provide backpacks for students in need. They have also partnered with the city of Fishers to create an online portal that allows teachers to request guest speakers, panelists, internships for students, project-based learning experiences and service-based learning. HSE student organizations have also partnered with food services to reduce the school's environmental impact by creating single-stream recycling.

partnering program that can leverage energy efficiency across
school districts (2021).

Green School Safety and Supervision Considerations

Outdoor Areas

Safety in a green school will likely focus on outdoor areas, such
as an outdoor classroom, gardens and play space. If the school is
considering creating an outdoor space, there are a few items to
keep in mind:

- ◆ The space should have active and quiet areas if a wide
  variety of activities will occur.
- ◆ Accessible spaces are needed for students with physical
  limitations.
- ◆ A sheltered space that provides shade and protection
  from the weather is needed, especially if students will
  use the space for an extended time.
- ◆ Accessible drinking water and fair proximity to a bath-
  room is needed (these are important if supervision is
  required).
- ◆ An accessible storage space for equipment might be
  needed.

When incorporating climbing equipment, rubber or bark mulch,
sand or rubber tiles can be used as surface material, with each
material having advantages and disadvantages (the rubber
mulch and tiles can be made from recycled tires). For shock
absorption, the surface fill material should be at least 12 inches
deep. Hypoallergenic and antimicrobial surfaces will help children with allergies. Supervision will be needed when students
are using the equipment, and there should be a hand-washing
opportunity afterward.

If students will be outside for an extended period, sun
exposure should be limited. The intensity of the sun's rays will
depend upon the time of the year and where you are located

(altitude and latitude). Wearing sunglasses, a hat and sunscreen will help students be more prepared to have class outdoors, though shade will need to be provided.

Natural outdoor play or learning spaces can use native trees and plants along with other structures to create an inviting area where students can spend a large portion of their day. These "multiple use" spaces encourage students to enjoy nature and use their surroundings as part of the learning process (Chan et al., 2015, p. 122). Schools that are located near the woods or other natural habitats such as lakes, streams, grasslands, etc. will want to consider the types of plants or animals that could be dangerous. For example, after a heavy rain, streams can flood their banks, include large branches and have a swift current. Walking paths should be designed to avoid poisonous plants such as poison ivy, oak or sumac. Students should be taught how to identify local poisonous plants as well.

Another important aspect of safety (and health) focuses on the products used to clean equipment and tools both indoors and outdoors. The Environmental Protection Agency (EPA) and non-profit organizations have created lists of green products that have been certified by either EcoLogo or Green Seal, which are independent certification organizations (2021). Please see the resource list at the end of the book for further information on cleaning products.

In upper grade levels, get the students involved in making decisions about safety. For example, students could evaluate how safely bus drop-offs and departures are handled. They can observe processes, collect and analyze data and present ideas to the faculty and administrations. Other safety audits can be conducted by students, such as outdoor social or play space or accessibility of school grounds. At Vienna International School, a design working station is used by secondary students to design and create sustainable products as part of a Green STEM unit. Safety is a focus in this room, with a large safety poster, items put away and stations cleaned after use.

Increasing walkers or bikers as a way to commute back and forth to school has safety issues and requires thoughtful

CREDIT Marti Hendrichs, Vienna International School

consideration. The National Center for Safe Routes to School (NCSR) can help with creating a walk or bike to school event (2021) as they provide training, guidelines, a data-collection system and examples that schools can use to address safety needs. Examples of safety improvements that a school can use include the following:

♦ Install raised crosswalks with high-visibility striping.
♦ Include new school-zone signage.
♦ Install traffic calming devices such as a roundabout or road diet.
♦ Install speed cameras in school zones.
♦ Employ rapid flashing beacons.
♦ Install sidewalks or crosswalks with flashers.
♦ Incorporate bike lanes.
♦ Increase or use crossing guards or safety officers in high-traffic areas (Brittin et al., 2015).

It is helpful to know where students live in relation to the school when making decisions about where to include walker and biker safety improvements. When students live fairly close to the school (1 mile or 1.5 kilometers for walkers and 3 miles or 4.5 kilometers for bikers), they are more likely to actively commute.

Supervision

Outdoor supervision of students is different from indoor classroom management. Supervision should be considered when setting up an outdoor space. Teachers should physically position themselves to maximize their sightline. Listening carefully will also help teachers in supervising a large space. The age of students will factor in to how much supervision is required as upper elementary students will need less oversight than preschool children. The National Program for Playground Safety (NPPS) provides professional development, educational materials and best-practice frameworks to support teachers and administrators (2021).

Diversity, Equity and Inclusion and Green Schools

The educational gap between students of color and Caucasian students is exacerbated by three important factors, "namely, educational deficits are cumulative, they are accelerated in the summer, and these accumulating deficits are not limited to cognitive skills" (Camasso & Jagannathan, 2018, p. 264). As children progress through the educational system, summer

Woodside Priory San Mateo, California Outdoor Education Experiences

The Priory Sustainability Club organizes and leads outdoor activities and habitat restoration. Students have also helped to build a 900-gallon recirculating aquaponics system, a living wall and a chicken enclosure where 50 chickens eat the school kitchen's prep waste. Class retreats include campus service projects, sustainable food sourcing in the school's garden, habitat restoration and off-site organic farming. New trees and bushes were planted on a highly erodible slope, and birdhouses and owl boxes were built to increase local and native wildlife on the campus. At least 200 minutes of physical education occurs each week, mainly outside, and Outdoor and Environmental Education courses are offered as elective courses. In spirituality classes, students conduct silent nature walks and conduct outdoor meditations. Many of the Priory teachers take students outside for teachable moments.

gaps and varying levels of access to school resources impact not only academics but also other non-cognitive skills, such as self-confidence, motivation and perseverance (Heckman, 2013). Research has shown that schools can increase student performance, especially when focused on environmental and ecological teaching (Clark, 2012). As well, "gardens increase student achievement through the creation of (a) a readiness to learn; (b) a resiliency in effort; and (c) an inculcation of personal responsibility and ownership" (Camasso & Jagannathan, 2018, p. 266).

Connecting students to the beauty and wonder of the natural world is part of how schools can support Diversity, Equity and Inclusion (DEI). Inquisitiveness, curiosity and imagination all play a role in sustainability teaching that, when combined with problem-based learning, can promote a true connection with nature (Levine & Zimmerman, 2010: Lieberrman & Hoody, 1998). A study that highlighted Nurture through Nature (NtN) found that the following components help to lessen the challenges of students' lives:

◆ Small class sizes
◆ Individualized tutoring
◆ High-quality instruction
◆ After-school and summer programs aligned with the school curriculum
◆ High levels of student attendance and participation
◆ Involved parents
◆ Hands-on learning opportunities in environmental and natural sciences
◆ An intervention of sufficient duration to insure maximum dosage (Camasso & Jagannathan, 2018, p. 274).

As much as green schools can support DEI, structural change is needed to address inequality. For example, many European Union (EU) countries (e.g., Greece, Germany, Austria, Hungary and Portugal), Latin American countries (e.g., Argentina, Chile, Mexico and Uruguay), Asian countries (e.g., China, India, and Vietnam) and the U.S. segregate sec-ondary school students through "tracking" (Gutiérrez et al., 2019). When tracking is used, students are typically evaluated and ranked prior to being separated into low, medium and high achievement levels. One of the main issues with tracking is that people of color and low-income students make up the majority of the low-track students while the high-achievement track tends to be students who have higher socioeconomic standing (Chong, 2018). To create systemic equity, at the very least, there needs to be a common core of learning outcomes in secondary schools (grades 6–12) as there is in primary edu-cation (grades PreK–5).

Green schools can go beyond this common core of learning outcomes by incorporating students' cultures, life experiences, languages and communities into not only all discipline areas but the school culture as well. This process needs to be authentic and valued to be truly embedded into daily school life. Creating green schools in equitable ways, including the distribution of federal funding that prioritizes schools in need of renova-tion and infrastructure repair, is needed. Interestingly, research shows "that shares of African-American and Hispanic students in schools and in the communities are statistically significant and positively associated with higher likelihood of new schools being green" (Zhao et al., 2019, p. 2234). Large urban schools are more likely to be green than non-urban, with schools that have prekindergarten programs the most likely to be a green school. The strongest indicator for new schools to be built as a green school is "neighborhood educational attainment" (Zhao et al., 2019, p. 2238), which means the higher the community educa-tion levels, the more likely a green school will be chosen when building a new school.

One way to better understand how your school is doing in relation to DEI is to conduct an equity audit. The goal of an equity audit is to better understand if there are discrepancies in institutional practices. It is important to understand how the access is to "grade-appropriate assignments, strong instruction, deep engagement, and high expectations" (The New Teacher

Project, 2018, p. 60). The focus of an equity audit includes programs, teaching quality and achievement. Equity questions include the following:

- ◆ Programmatic Equity
  - Which population groups are underrepresented in Advanced Placement classes or honors classes?
  - Which groups are overrepresented or underrepresentation in special education classes?
  - Which groups are disciplined more often and more severely than other groups?
- ◆ Teaching Quality
  - Are the most experienced teachers teaching the students with the greatest needs?
  - Are most of the new teachers teaching in the schools with the greatest needs?
  - Are there certain schools where there is high teacher mobility? Why?
  - Are teachers in the high need's areas, like special education and bilingual education, certified?
- ◆ Achievement Equity
  - Where are the achievement and opportunity gaps among population groups based on the state assessment exam at each grade level?
  - Which population groups are graduating at lower rates than others?
  - Which students are being retained in grade?
  - Which students are dropping out of school? (Intercultural Development Research Association, 2021, para 11).

Once the equity audit is completed, administrators and teachers can review the data to better understand where gaps can be found. There is no "quick fix" to inequitable allocation, though the time spent on addressing systemic choices and decisions will be well worth the investment.

Conclusions

Much of the U.S. school infrastructure is more than 40 years old and needs either to be torn down or heavily modernized. New state and national policies are long overdue to support an equitable distribution of funds and resources to public PreK–12 schools. As COVID-19 has negatively impacted the teaching process, many schools have turned to using the outdoors as a learning tool as it is cost-effective and include access to fresh air. As school districts have a wide latitude in adopting more environmental policies, teachers, students and the local community can request better air filtration, the use of sustainable cleaning materials and the promotion of health and wellness within schools. One way to fund these initiatives is to leverage purchasing power by working with other school districts. Teachers are not typically involved in educational policy, though having their voice on a state educator advisory council would be a way to involve them more in policy decisions. Teachers can also play a role in incorporating Diversity, Equity and Inclusion (DEI) by connecting students to the natural world through sustainability teaching. Embedding students' life experiences, cultures and languages in the school culture will show students they are valued.

Questions to Consider

- ◆ In what way could you become more involved in policy decisions within your school district, local or state government?
- ◆ What changes would you like to see made to make your school more sustainable?
- ◆ What steps could you make in achieving some of these sustainability ideas?
- ◆ Does your school district leverage its purchasing power to save money? If not, how could you support this process?

References

Brittin, J., Sorensen, D., Trowbridge, M., Lee, K. K., Breithecker, D., Frerichs, L., & Huang, T. (2015). *Physical activity design guidelines for school architecture.* https://journals.plos.org/plosone/article?id=10.1371/journal.pone.0132597.

Camasso, M., & Jagannathan, R. (2018). Improving academic outcomes in poor urban schools through nature-based learning. *Cambridge Journal of Education, 48*(2), 263–277.

Center for Green Schools. (2018). *School sustainability leaders network.* https://centerforgreenschools.org/school-sustainability-leaders-network.

Chan, T. C., Mense, E. G., Lane, K. E., & Richardson, M. D. (2015). *Marketing the green school: Form, function, and the future.* IGI Global.

Chong, P. W. (2018). The Finnish "recipe" towards inclusions: Concocting educational equity, policy rigour, and proactive support structures. *Scandinavian Journal of Educational Research, 62*(4), 501–518.

Clark, P. (2012). *Education for sustainability: Becoming naturally smart.* Routledge.

Duffett, A., Farkas, S., Rotherman, A., & Silva, E. 2008. *Waiting to be won over: Teachers speak on the profession, unions, and reform.* Education Sector Report.

Goodall, J. (n.d.). https://www.janegoodall.org/.

Green Schools Alliance. (2021). *GSA district collaborative.* https://www.greenschoolsalliance.org/program/districts.

Green Schoolyards America. (2021). *National COVID-19 outdoor learning initiative.* https://www.greenschoolyards.org/covid-learn-outside.

Gutiérrez, G., Jerrim, J., & Torres, R. (2019). School segregation across the world: Has any progress been made in reducing the separation of the rich from the poor? *The Journal of Economic Inequality, 18,* 157–179.

Heckman, J. J. (2013). *Giving kids a fair chance.* MIT Press.

Intercultural Development Research Association. (2021). *Using equity audits to assess and address opportunity gaps across education.* Equity Audit Questions.

Levine, P. B., & Zimmerman, D. S. (2010). *Targeting investments in children: Fighting poverty when resources are limited.* University of Chicago Press.

Lieberrman, G. A., & Hoody, L. L. (1998). *Closing the achievement gap: Using the environment as an integrating context for learning – results of a national study*. Council of Chief State School Officers, Executive Summary.

National Center for Safe Routes to School. (2021). *Safe routes*. http://www.saferoutesinfo.org/.

National Program for Playground Safety. (2021). *Playground supervision*. https://playgroundsafety.org/.

The New Teacher Project. (2018). *The opportunity myth*. https://tntp.org/.

Rainwater, B., & Hartke, J. (2011). *Local leaders in sustainability: Special report from Sundance (A national action plan for greening America's school)*. The American Institute of Architects and the U.S. Green Building Council, Inc.

U.S. Department of Energy. (2021). *K–12 solutions for building energy excellence*. https://betterbuildingssolutioncenter.energy.gov/.

U.S. Environmental Protection Agency. (2021). *Safer choice*. https://www.epa.gov/saferchoice.

USGBC. (2010). *Greening our schools: A state legislator's guide to best policy practices*. State Legislative Summit.

Zhao, S., Zhou, S., & Noonan, D. S. (2019). Environmental justice and green schools: Assessing students and communities' access to green schools. *Social Science Quarterly*, *100*(6), 2223–2239.

8

Cost Benefits of Green Schools and How to Leverage Funding and Partnerships

"Time spent among the trees is never time wasted."

Anonymous

Vignette

Ms. Baker was frustrated that the fundraising for the water-bottle station project she and the Green Team had been focused on since the start of the school year wasn't making much progress. They had raised a few hundred dollars from a bake sale, but it wasn't enough to buy even one bottle station. As she sat reviewing various fundraising websites, she stumbled upon a site that had fundraising ideas such as selling refillable water bottles at school (https://www.h2oforlifeschools.org/page/fundraising-ideas). Another site shared links to grants based on individual states that could provide funding (http://becausewater.com/grants-water-bottle-filling-stations/). Ms. Baker's frustration was ebbing away as she realized there were more opportunities to get the funds needed for the three water bottle stations than she realized. She quickly sent an email to the Green Team to set up a meeting for the next afternoon.

DOI: 10.4324/9781003164524-8

Chapter Objectives

♦ Describe the cost benefits of green schools.
♦ Share information on grant funding to support sustainability.
♦ Explain how to leverage partnerships with governmental agencies, non-profits and/or companies.
♦ Highlight low- or no-cost ways to be sustainable.
♦ Discuss how green schools impact the local community.

Cost Benefits of Green Schools

The U.S. and many other nations have free and universal public education that instills democratic values such as fairness and cooperation. The main goal of PreK–12 education is to create citizens that can contribute to our democratic society. School buildings and grounds are places where students meet, interact and learn about the world. These spaces need to be safe, healthy and aesthetically pleasing and include flexible areas for project-based work and collaborative learning. It is incredibly important that this setting show students and teachers that the community values them and education. Alas, in many school districts, this is not the case.

Of the approximate 130,000 public school buildings in the U.S., over 50% of public school districts need to update or replace their PreK–12 buildings (Congressional Research Service, 2020). Each of these 130,000 buildings has a lifespan of 50 to 60 years, so the types of materials and resources used to build these structures will have an incredible environmental impact for decades to come. The cost of a green school is only slightly higher than a conventional building and can save money over the lifetime of the building. The financial benefits of green schools are 20 times greater than conventional schools (Kats, 2006) as they use a third less energy and water, reduce pollution, have less maintenance costs and reduce the stress on the energy grid (Filardo, 2021). With just energy management, U.S. schools could see a savings of at least 25% off utility costs, which is about $3 billion a year.

Typically, conventional schools are built to meet the minimum standards, which decreases the initial cost of a building. Although, what isn't taken into consideration is comfort, productivity and the healthy work environment for those who work in this space. Data collected in conventional school buildings show unhealthy air, poor ventilation, poor aesthetics and minimally comfortable rooms, which increase illness and bring down test scores (American Society of Civil Engineers, 2021). In a 2006 report that reviewed 30 green schools, it was shown that green schools cost slightly more than conventional schools (approximately 2%), but over the life of the building, it can improve teacher retention, lower health costs, lower energy and water costs, reduce student and teacher absenteeism and cut down on pollution (Katz). Table 8.1 shows the breakdown of financial benefits of building a green school.

Another cost benefit of green schools is decreased health risks and insurance impacts. Because of the improved indoor environmental quality, green schools have lower health claims and worker compensation. For example, schools that have mold or asbestos will pay higher insurance costs. If a school building was built before 1981, there is a high likelihood that it has asbestos (U.S. EPA, 2003). Green schools have improved ventilation and go through a commissioning process, which requires that the building systems are designed, installed and tested based on

TABLE 8.1 Financial benefits of building a green school

Financial Benefits of Green Schools ($/ft^2)	
Energy	$9
Emissions	$1
Water and Wastewater	$49
Increased Earnings	$3
Asthma Reduction	$3
Cold and Flu Reductio	$5
Teacher Retention	$4
Employment Impact	$2
Total	$74
Cost of Greening	($3)
Net Financial Benefits	$71

(Kats, 2006, p. 2).

specific standards. The green school's plant manager is trained to efficiently operate these systems to improve air quality and occupant comfort as well as reduce maintenance costs. Typically, these green schools will have completed LEED certification (discussed in Chapter 6). Within school LEED certification,

> prerequisites and credits focus on seven types of risk: property loss, general liability, business interruption, vehicular, health and workers comp, life and environmental liability. Of the 64 LEED points available (not including innovation credits), 49 (77%) are associated with measures that have potential risk-reduction benefits. (Kats, 2006, pp. 18–19)

LEED certification can also be a valuable tool in relation to climate change. Approximately half of U.S. PreK–12 schools are in high-flood-risk areas, and one-third of them are "geographically prone to heat waves and tornados" (National Center for Disaster Preparedness, 2021, para. 2). Internationally, higher-than-average temperatures can have a negative relationship on educational attainment, especially in the tropics (Randell & Gray, 2019). Green schools can lesson climate change issues by deriving their energy from renewable sources that are physically on school property. If schools are in areas where climate change will have more of an impact, they can be modernized to "protect lives and reduce the level of relief funding needed following disasters" (Filardo, 2021, p. 11). For example, natural disasters such as high-heat days or severe storms can be mitigated by green technology features such as spray foam insulation. In hurricane-prone areas, replacing windows and roofs to withstand high winds, and in fire-prone spaces, including fire-resistant roofs, creating a defensible space around buildings and updating the ventilation system to filter smoke or use portable air cleaners can help a great deal in combatting these climate issues (Seyedin et al., 2020).

School structures are not only used as safe spaces but also provide a setting for quality learning to take place. As discussed in Chapter 6, student performance can be impacted by a building's physical setting. Consider where you are sitting right now. How is the air temperature, lighting and air quality? Are you struggling to read what is on the page due to low lighting, or are you too warm, which is causing you to not pay attention? Maybe it is noisy outside and it is impacting your ability to focus. It is easy to see how your environment can impact your attention and concentration levels. Classrooms need to be individualized to consider the class as a whole and each particular student's viewpoint. Research shows that students who have quality space with appropriate lighting, temperature, individualization and appropriate stimulation levels perform 17% better than students without these environmental aspects, even when controlling for socioeconomic status (Barrett et al., 2017). North Park School for Innovation took a dreary courtyard (Photo 8.1) and created a green space that students could view from their classrooms. The renovated courtyard is an interactive garden (Photo 8.2).

CREDIT Jeff Cacek, Stan Mraz, North Park School for Innovation

CREDIT Jeff Cacek, Stan Mraz, North Park School for Innovation

Quality school environments can only be maintained with adequate funding. As of 2019, 77% of school funding came from local revenue, and this figure continues to increase. At the state level, from 2009–2019, funds for capital projects and debt service to school districts have continually decreased from $16.4 billion to $9.7 billion, which is approximately a 30% decrease (American Society of Civil Engineers, 2021). "Only eight states provide 50% or more to local districts for school construction capital outlay and debt service, and there are eleven states that provide no dedicated construction funding or debt service" (U.S. Census of Governments, 2020). The support of PreK–12 educational facilities at the federal level is even worse. The U.S. Department of Education has no dedicated office to provide support to PreK–12 school districts or states on school facilities data. Also, federal funding for PreK–12 school facilities was only about 1.3% or 7.1 billion in 2020 (Congressional Research Service, 2020). During COVID-19, the Elementary and Secondary School Emergency Relief (ESSER) funds helped with school operating costs. About $31 billion was used by schools for annual maintenance and operations, including air-filtration systems, cleaning supplies, signage and testing infrastructure.

As essentially all PreK–12 schools, including green schools, are dependent on local, state and federal funding, it is imperative that system reforms occur, including the following:

♦ Enact state legislation to provide school districts the flexibility to raise revenue from sources other than property tax.
♦ Establish dedicated state revenue streams for repayment of PreK–12 capital improvement bonds.
♦ Facilitate close partnerships between PreK–12 school districts and community colleges and universities.
♦ Establish a federal-state partnership with a PreK–12 infrastructure "revolving fund."
♦ Incorporate public school infrastructure in any federal infrastructure initiative.
♦ Establish federal programs to fund states for capital construction for PreK–12 infrastructure (Filardo, 2021, p. 51).

At the PreK–12 level, a priority to improve facilities management needs to occur, including the following:

♦ Incorporate the values and vision for adequate and equitable school buildings and grounds into the school district's mission, vision and strategic plans.
♦ Establish regular lines of communication between school district program/curriculum staff and facilities staff.
♦ Provide relevant building-condition system data to facilities maintenance and operations personnel.

- Provide adequate staff training and ongoing technical support for facilities staff.
- Conduct facilities workshops for teachers, parents, students (if appropriate) and community members about facilities planning and decision-making (Filardo, 2021, p. 52).

Grant Funding and How to Stretch a Budget

Teachers, administrators or other school staff members who are interested in beginning the green school development process will need to consider funding and how to find financial resources. There are numerous options, though it will depend on the size of the PreK–12 school, types of projects being considered and how much time school members are able to give to the process. If you just want to take on small-scale projects initially, then ad hoc sources may be the best opportunity for funding. This could include submitting a short proposal to the Parent-Teacher Association (PTA) or the principal, who likely have discretionary funds ($50–$150) that can be used. No matter what the size of the project, think about who might have close ties to what is being planned. For example, if the goal is to create a school garden, local landscape nurseries might be willing to give a discount or donate plants. If you want to buy a solar panel ($40–$100) that will be used to educate students about how the panel works, then a home improvement-retailer might offer discounts. You should talk with your school district's purchasing manager as they will likely have local organizations that they have done business with and might know who would be willing to donate supplies.

Other opportunities to stretch a small budget is to ask students, parents and community members to volunteer their time. Many people are willing to spend a Saturday morning creating a garden plot, weeding, creating a mulch trail or painting. If money is needed for supplies, a fundraising event may be the answer. There are numerous ways to raise $500 or more through an email donation request, online gift card selling, a request to businesses to match school or donated funds, a raffle or selling school merchandise. The fundraising process can become an educational opportunity as well. If more funds are needed or you are trying to install a renewable energy system, a state utility grant (https://www.dsireusa.org/ or your state's Division of Energy Resources) would be a good option. Many utilities assign an account manager to school districts, so contact the school district treasurer to see if your district has one as they can help navigate utility incentive programs.

Grants and Resources

There are numerous foundations and companies that support sustainability efforts (see resource list at the end of the book for more information). Typically, there is a grant cycle each year with proposals due early in the school year, though each foundation is different. For example, the U.S. EPA (https://www.epa.gov/education/grants) supports environmental education projects, with each region of the country having a resource person that can be contacted for questions. If you are considering grants over $1,000, it is a good idea to have evidence that you can successfully complete an environmental project. This could entail a smaller project (e.g., creating birdhouses or a walking path with signage) that you have already implemented. For large grants ($25,000 or more), you will likely need principal or school district approval. It is also a good idea to communicate your plans to the administration so that they can potentially give feedback and maybe help with funding support. Mid to large school districts should have someone in the district office that can help with grant proposals and paperwork (e.g., banking accounts and tax information).

As energy is the second-highest operating expenditure (after teacher's salaries), there are numerous incentives to incorporate energy-efficient systems in PreK–12 schools. The U.S. Department of Energy (DOE) has also created the Better Buildings Challenge, with a goal to "improve the energy efficiency of buildings by at least 20% over 10 years" (Borgeson & Zimring, 2013). More information about this program and the resources available are at https://betterbuildingssolutioncenter. energy.gov/challenge. Power purchase agreements (PPAs) is

TABLE 8.2 How a green school could obtain funding for renewable energy

Multisource Example for Renewable Energy	
Local Donations	$4,500
Utility Rebate (from energy company)	$3,500
First year energy savings (more efficient system)	$2,500
Existing school budget	$2,500
School District Contribution	$3,000
State grant	$5,000
Total funding	$21,000

(Kats, 2006, p. 2).

another way that schools can benefit from renewable energy without up-front costs. With a PPA, a third party owns, operates and maintains the system, and the school pays a prenegotiated rate for the power. In table 8.2, a multisource model is shared, which offers one example of how a green school could obtain funding for renewable energy.

Partnerships That Can Support Green School Projects

Human capital, such as a person's expertise and skills, can be used in developing green school projects. These skills may come from the Green Team members, school staff, volunteers, community members or local businesses. Strong partnerships within the school (e.g., administration and teachers, PTA and school staff) and outside the school (e.g., non-profit organizations, businesses,

North Park School for Innovation, Columbia Heights, Minnesota Cost Savings

Initially resistant to spending funds on compostable garbage bags and recycle bins, the North Park Elementary School District Office realized that over time they would have a cost benefit. North Park's principal and science teacher focus on an energy-saving project each year, which also saves money over time. Some of those projects have included solar panels, rain gardens and edible schoolyards. A biodigester was installed, which turns food scraps, milk cartons and paper towels into compost material and saves on landfill waste. Once the biomass boiler is installed, the biodigester's compost will be used to heat the school building. This is likely the first school of its kind to essentially use compost to heat a school building!

parks) are crucial for a green school to be successful (Sterrett et al., 2014). These partnerships can help with resources, materials or provide intellectual capital, which will strengthen sustainability projects and initiatives. Schools can also develop a formal commitment with a university, business or organization with a memorandum of understanding. Typically, this type of arrangement is developed when substantial volunteer time or business facilities are being used. Informal arrangements might include monthly meetings or volunteer time, though that depends upon the size and scope of the project.

Research has shown that developing a relationship between a university and a PreK–12 school has considerable benefits for students (Washington et al., 2019). Connections between schools have also been found to be an effective way to quickly learn about new initiatives or ideas. There are also a number of online teacher communities that focus on sustainability (https://naaee.org/eepro/groups), with focus on climate change, conservation, E-STEM, K–12 EE, etc. When setting up a partnership, consider the following items:

- ◆ Establish goals for the partnership. What do you want to accomplish?
- ◆ Decide who will be the project lead from each institution and how communication will occur between groups.
- ◆ How frequently will you meet, and who will join the discussion?
- ◆ What performance outcomes or impact of the partnership will be monitored?
- ◆ What type of funding is needed, who will contribute and how will the funds be dispersed?
- ◆ What is the timeline for achieving the goals?

Finding experts that can help support development, programming and projects will fast-track initiatives. Typically, these experts will volunteer their time, though occasionally, a small stipend might be needed.

Partnerships that occur within the school can also be a powerful way to gain support for sustainability initiatives. For example, it would be helpful to have at least one member of the cafeteria staff on the Green Team. This person can keep lines of communication open in relation to food sourcing, food waste, composting, the school garden, etc. Though where food is sourced will likely be decided at the school district level, cafeteria staff should have input into what is being served for breakfast and lunch and how waste is handled.

Low- or No-Cost Ways to Be Sustainable

For schools that have a limited budget, there are low-cost ways to promote environmental projects. If your school doesn't have a Green Team, see Chapter 3 for more information about setting one up. This team can actively engage with the school and local community on numerous initiatives, such as a recycling-bin decorating con-test, school-grounds monthly trash pickup or a progress tracker on how much food was composted or items that were recycled. A repurpose fair where students and parents exchange books or clothes would be another low-cost sustainable initiative. Once the Green Team is established, make sure that you have open communication with administration.

All decisions that impact the entire school should be discussed with administrators early on in the decision-making process as they have an overall understanding of school processes that teachers and staff might not know about. For example, if the Green Team is interested in incorporating more locally sourced

Gove Elementary, Belle Glade, Florida, and Legacy Elementary, Madison, Alabama Multiple Partnerships and Funding Sources

Legacy Elementary has plants donated by home-improvement chains and received fish for their pond from the Alabama Outdoor Wildlife Federation. They also receive a budget from the school. A STEAM class was created at Gove Elementary with a Horace Mann grant. With support from the Everglades Foundation, Loggerhead Marine Life and the University of Florida and support from local bee keepers and farmers, the school has a diversity of partnerships and funding. Both of these schools have dedicated parents, students and community support to allow for strong sustainability projects to be developed.

food into cafeteria meals, the school principal can help with understanding how the school district purchasing process works. If, after a conversation with the principal, the Green Team finds that it isn't possible to buy locally sourced food (at this time), the Green Team might be able to incorporate a composting project instead. Composting essentially requires a small plot of land where non-animal scraps can be buried. This type of project should include student leadership as the entire student population will need to learn what can and cannot be composted. For at least the first few weeks of the school year, students can be taught how to monitor the trash and compost bins at breakfast and lunch. Including this project in the curriculum would

CREDIT Jeff Cacek, Stan Mraz, North Park School for Innovation

give all incoming students the opportunity to learn about the initiative and participate. In Photo 8.3, a student at North Park School for Innovation is using the cafeteria system for recycling, composting and biodigester materials so there is very little that goes to the landfill.

Recycling is another low-cost activity, which surprisingly doesn't occur in a number of schools. If your school is currently recycling paper, plastic and aluminum, there are other items that organizations are interested in collecting. For example, Crayola will recycle dried markers and broken crayons (https://www.crayola.com/colorcycle), and TerraCycle will recycle chip bags, pens, applesauce pouches, candy wrappers, batteries, art supplies and many more items (https://www.terracycle.com/en-US/). Recycling can be incorporated into the school's curriculum as well, as the students will need to be taught which items are reusable or in need of recycling and where they should be deposited. If it isn't doable for every teacher to take this project on, the Green Team and custodial staff can control recycling. Finally, the Green Team should do a trash audit a few times a year, which includes choosing random classrooms, staff offices and the cafeteria to provide an in-depth look at what is thrown away. For example, if the Green Team finds a lot of candy wrappers or Lunchable plastic containers, teachers could build healthy eating concepts into their curriculum.

Other low-cost projects include acquiring indoor plants for the school. The Green Team could ask parents, teachers, staff and the local community (including landscape nurseries and flower shops) to donate easy-to-grow plants such as spider, pothos, jade, English ivy or snake plants. Plants have been shown to purify the air and improve behavior. Gardening is another project that could be fairly low cost, especially if materials and seeds are donated from local businesses. Installing a few rain barrels to catch rainwater would also provide a low-cost way to water the garden.

In relation to energy, it is better to use daylight in classrooms as students perform better than when using conventional lighting (it also cuts down on energy costs). The following are additional low-cost ideas:

Energy

♦ Have your energy supplier conduct an energy audit. It should be a free service and will provide the Green Team a better understanding of the school's energy efficiency. The audit could also be used by teachers interested in discussing energy sources, energy efficiency and clean energy.

♦ Encourage personal responsibility among teachers and staff for them to turn off all technology at night, turn off lights when outside the room and close doors.

♦ Use weather stripping and caulk to increase room insulation.

♦ Make the school community aware of their energy use by posting signage in high-traffic areas of how much energy is used in the school each month. The Green Team could also post carbon dioxide and sulfur dioxide footprints for the school as well. Again, this is something that could be used be teachers, especially after a year of data has been collected.

Water

♦ Install low-flow water aerators in bathrooms (fairly inexpensive).

♦ Landscaping should include drought resistant and native plants that require less water.

♦ Install a rain tank and/or rain barrels for irrigation.

Safe Materials and Healthy Air

♦ Begin using green cleaning products. This may take time as the school may have a large cleaning supply on hand.

♦ Use natural fertilizers (manure, compost) rather than artificial ones and non-chemical pesticides such as peppermint, lemon or orange (ants and roaches) and cedarwood (lice).

♦ Separate chemical storage from the HVAC systems.

Green Schools and the Impact on the Local Community

Schools are extensions of their community, with social, financial and political ties to businesses, organizations, parents and other schools. Using events and social media to engage with the local community, schools can share their mission and initiatives to help others better understand what they are trying to accomplish. For example, homecoming, sporting events, education fairs, school orientation, farmer's markets or art fairs can provide an opportunity to highlight fundraising or request help for sustainability initiatives. Using student leadership and participation will also increase parent interest. An important part of the school's connection to the community is the sense of place that the school can create, which includes its infrastructure.

As part of the American Jobs Plan (AJP), which was passed by the U.S. Senate in August 2021, an investment of $100 billion to upgrade and build new PreK–12 public schools was included (Committee for a Responsible Federal Budget, 2021). These funds will help transform the public school system and should connect to sustainability initiatives such as incorporating renewable energy. Every community will likely be impacted by the AJP, which should stimulate local economies, especially in helping to eliminate the inequities that currently plague urban and rural public school districts. For example, there are school districts that receive less funding from local property taxes, which are the main source of revenue that schools use to upgrade and maintain facilities.

Colegio Santa Francesca Romana, Bogota, Colombia and Parkway School District, Chesterfield, Missouri

Supporting the Local Community

The students at Colegio Santa Francisca Romana – "Pachas," a K–12 all-girls school, wanted to empower women to take sustainable actions. The students helped with the restoration of the Bogotá River ecosystem, which has significant pollution due to the population density in the surrounding area. They held a fundraising campaign and bought trees to plant near the river. The students also supported the foundation that works on the river with food during the pandemic. At Parkway School District, there is a district wellness committee made up of parents, students, staff and community members that create health and wellness initiatives with the support of wellness leaders. High school students in the district also have an annual Day of Service, where the students explore environmental issues such as wildlife preservation or water pollution.

This is a cycle that negatively impacts the neighborhoods where these schools reside as parents are not interested in sending their children to schools in disrepair, so they look elsewhere to live. With less tax base to use, these schools fall further and further behind in infrastructure upgrades, which ultimately hurts their community.

Consider how upgrading PreK–12 school infrastructure can affect local communities. "Every $1 billion of public funding spent on construction generates 17,785 jobs" (Bivens & Blair, 2016, para. 32). These are construction, supplier, maintenance, design, clean energy and other jobs that positively impact communities. Schools are also uniquely positioned to serve as models for clean-energy technology. Once these energy upgrades are completed, the cost savings can potentially be used to increase teacher and staff salaries. Another school upgrade that is needed is transitioning the aging school bus fleet to zero emission. School buses, which are typically powered by diesel fuel, produce more powerful pollutants than petrol vehicles. These pollutants can negatively impact children when the buses are idling by schools as well as when children are riding inside (Solomon et al., 2001). Upgrading to zero-emission buses would not only improve community air quality but also benefit the health of students.

The physical and emotional health of teachers is another important aspect of upgrading PreK–12 public schools. Teachers live in the neighborhoods surrounding the schools and are an important component of a healthy and prosperous community. It is estimated that urban school districts can spend, on average, $20,000 for every new teacher hired, which includes recruitment, hiring, training and separation. If teachers are leaving the school district within one to two years due to poor working conditions, schools are not receiving a good return on investment (Learning Policy Institute, 2017). Upgraded green buildings can help teachers deal with some of the stressors of teaching, such as poor air quality, inadequate heating and cooling systems, crowded hallways and an unwelcoming color and space.

School quality is an important consideration for families trying to decide which community to settle in. A green school can help to increase property values by incorporating a greater demand for one neighborhood over another (Neilsen & Zimmerman, 2011). This positive impact on home prices will also increase tax revenue, which, over time, can help to pay for the school renovations. Once the green school is established, community members can help students better understand the functions of building. For example, landscape architects can conduct research with students on soil, native plants and wild-life, and students can work with energy experts on the use of solar panels or geothermal systems. The green school can also "encourage business investment and job creation, and serve as the cornerstone of vibrant communities" (Center for Green Schools, 2018, para. 4).

Green Schools Create Jobs

Modernizing, retrofitting and building green schools will take major effort, especially in areas that have low wealth. "Taking up this work will create and provide good jobs, helping strengthen and revitalize the economies of struggling communities" (Filardo, 2021, p. 11). It is estimated that if the capital construction gap of $57 billion (annually) were closed, almost a million jobs would be created (Bivens & Blair, 2016). Green jobs will be needed to retrofit school HVAC systems to include renewable energy sources such as solar panels, geothermal system or wind turbines. Local construction workers can work on the backlog of renovations and capital construction projects, which will also support manufacturers and suppliers. Once these renovated or new school buildings are completed, families will be attracted to the community and then contribute economically and socially, which strengthens the community even more.

Cleaning and maintaining facilities might not be the most glamorous jobs, though they are dependable jobs that contribute to the local economy. From 2017–2019, the maintenance and operations (M&O) costs of PreK–12 school buildings were approximately $56 billion per year (Filardo, 2021). Currently, there is an underinvestment for M&O of $27.6 billion. If M&O

were fully funded, an estimated 320,000 new jobs would be created across the U.S. (21st Century School Fund, 2018). These are direct and indirect jobs that would include construction workers, building engineers, architects, landscape designers and groundskeepers and health and safety officers.

Conclusions

A green school costs slightly more (approximately 2%) than a conventional school though, over the lifetime of the building, will save money, energy and water and will improve teacher retention, lower health costs and reduce student and teacher absenteeism. There are also less maintenance costs and pollution over time. Much of school funding comes from local revenue as state funds have continually decreased over the last decade. Systems funding reform would allow school districts flexibility to raise revenue from sources other than property taxes. Grants can provide funding support for school sustainability initiatives. Typically, grant funders require schools to submit a grant proposal explaining project goals and evaluation procedures. Low-cost ways to incorporate sustainability include recycling, composting, bringing plants into school, creating a garden or building rain barrels. There are also efficient, low-cost ways to reduce energy and water consumption. Upgrading PreK–12 school infrastructure can increase school quality, increase the number of families interested in living in that community and retain teachers over a longer period. Modernizing schools to include renewable energy, efficient systems and natural light will increase green jobs, which is good for the economy and supports communities.

Questions to Consider

♦ How old is your school building?
♦ Is it time to either modernize the structure or build a new building?

- ◆ Are there opportunities at your school to include low-cost ways to make the building more efficient, such as including composting?
- ◆ Are you interested in finding funding for a particular sustainability project? If so, review grant websites at the end of the book.

References

21st Century School Fund. (2018). *Forum guide to facility information management: 2018 update.* http://www.21csf.org/csf-home/view_ PubList.asp?rsview95Pub_PagingMove=1.

American Society of Civil Engineers. (2021). *Report card for America's infrastructure.* https://infrastructurereportcard.org/cat-item/schools/.

Barrett, P., Davies, F., Zhang, Y., & Barrett, L. (2017). The holistic impact of classroom spaces on learning in specific subjects. *Environment and Behavior, 49*(4), 425–451.

Bivens, J., & Blair, J. (2016). *A public investment agenda that delivers the goods for American workers needs to be long-lived, broad, and subject to democratic oversight.* Economic Policy Institute.

Borgeson, M., & Zimring, M. (2013). *Financing energy upgrades for K–12 school districts.* A Guide to Funding for Energy Efficiency and Renewable Energy Improvements.

Center for Green Schools. (2018). *Green school buildings are better for communities.* https://www.centerforgreenschools.org/green-sch ools-are-better-communities.

Committee for a Responsible Federal Budget. (2021). *What's in President Biden's American jobs plan?* https://www.crfb.org/blogs/ whats-president-bidens-american-jobs-plan.

Congressional Research Service. (2020). *School construction and renovation: A review of federal programs and legislation.* Congressional Research Service Report.

Filardo, M. (2021). *State of our schools: America's K–12 facilities 2021.* 21st Century School Fund.

Kats, G. (2006). *Greening America's schools: Cost and benefits. A capital E report.* https://www.usgbc.org/resources/greening-america039s-schools-costs-and-benefits.

Learning Policy Institute. (2017). *What's the cost of teacher turnover?* https://learningpolicyinstitute.org/product/the-cost-of-teacher-turnover.

National Center for Disaster Preparedness. (2021). *U.S. national hazards index*. https://ncdp.columbia.edu/library/mapsmapping-projects/us-natural-hazards-index/.

Neilsen, C., & Zimmerman, S. (2011). *The effect of school construction on test scores, school enrollment, and home prices*. The Institute for the Study of Labor.

Randell, H., & Gray, C. (2019). Climate change and educational attainment in the global tropics. *Proceedings of the National Academy of the Sciences of the U.S.A, 116*(18), 8840–8845.

Seyedin, H., Dowlati, M., Moslehi, S., & Sakaei, F. (2020). Health, safety, and education measures for fire in schools: A review article. *Journal of Education and Health Promotion, 121*(9). https://www.jehp.net/text.asp?2020/9/1/121/285165.

Solomon, G. M., Campbell, T. R., Feuer, G. R., Masters, J., Samkian, A., & Paul, K. A. (2001). *No breathing in the aisles: Diesel exhaust inside school buses*. National Resources Defense Council. https://www.nrdc.org/sites/default/files/schoolbus.pdf.

Sterrett, W. L., Imig, S., & Moore, D. (2014). U.S. department of education green ribbon schools: Leadership insights and implications. *Journal of Organizational Learning and Leadership, 12*(2), 1–18.

U.S. Census of Governments. (2020). *F-33 Fiscal Survey: State revenue for capital outlay and debt service FY2009–19*. State Funding for Schools.

U.S. EPA. (2003). *The ABCs of asbestos in schools*. www2.epa.gov/sites/production/files/documents/abcsfinal.pdf.

Washington, A. R., Goings, R. B., & Henfield, M. S. (Eds.). (2019). *Creating and sustaining effective K–12 school partnerships: Firsthand accounts of promising practices*. Information Age Publishing.

9

How to Evaluate Campus, Curriculum and Community Sustainability Initiatives

"The ultimate test of man's conscience may be his willingness to sacrifice something today for future generations whose words of thanks will not be heard."

Gaylord Nelson

Vignette

There has been a garden at Roosevelt Middle School for over a decade. Mrs. Willer, the Green Team coordinator, had noticed that many of the people in the garden were either retired teachers, parents or nature-center volunteers. Many of the teachers in the building did not use the garden in their curriculum projects or take their students out to experience the outdoor space. She wondered if the teachers had more say in preparing the garden area each year or if there were more opportunities beyond growing fruits and vegetables that they might be interested in participating. Mrs. Willer had some interesting ideas on next steps and planned to share them at the next Green Team meeting.

DOI: 10.4324/9781003164524-9

Chapter Objectives

♦ Explain evaluation and its use in a PreK–12 green school.
♦ Describe how to evaluate the interconnection of sustainability initiatives.
♦ Explain the evaluation process for both campus and curriculum sustainability initiatives.
♦ Highlight how community relationships should be evaluated to keep them healthy and meaningful.

Green School Evaluation: What Is It and How Can It Be Used?

We are barraged with information every day, some of it useful and some of it misleading and potentially harmful. These miscommunications can lead to the reinforcement of negative stereotypes, poor decision-making and mistrust of vetted, factual information. This chapter will discuss ways to conduct evaluation and carefully consider how to use the information to evaluate curriculum and campus sustainability initiatives and the relationships with the community and outside organizations. Evaluation is useful for the following reasons:

♦ It clarifies what students are learning and understanding in relation to the curriculum.
♦ It creates opportunities to provide funding agencies a description of the performance and effectiveness of initiatives.
♦ It provides information that supports improvement in future activities.
♦ It promotes professionalism in the Green School movement (Stokking et al., 1999, p. 9).

Many people think that evaluation is a difficult process, so they leave it out of their projects. This means there is no way to know whether the initiatives are effective or not. Evaluation is a crucial step in any project and, with just a little time and effort, can give you impactful information. First, let's consider what you want to accomplish. It can be assumed that you will establish goals for your sustainability projects and will need to know to what degree you are able to achieve these goals. We can also assume that student outcomes will play a key role in these goals, so we are now looking for those conditions that are facilitating output measures showing the effectiveness of the program (Verhelst et al., 2020). For example, in a green school, you would be looking for sustainability competencies that go beyond knowledge – such as holistic, action oriented and pluralistic (acceptance of different backgrounds and cultures) – and what conditions are enabling these outcomes to occur.

Many of us want to believe that because we have created an amazing curriculum unit or sustainability project, it will be effective and students will gain knowledge and skills and change misconceptions because of it. Unfortunately, just because we may think it is effective, that doesn't make it so. That is where evaluation comes in. Evaluation helps you to understand whether your students are achieving a high level of understanding, can critically think about sustainability issues and apply those concepts to complex situations. Incorporating evaluation into curriculum and campus initiatives will also show that you are an educator who wants to improve and hold yourself (and others) accountable for what you are doing.

Students, as much as possible, should be a part of the evaluation process. For them to be independent, critical thinkers, they must see that they have a voice in how the school and classroom operate. Establishing an atmosphere that is open, where everyone perceives their opinion to be worthy, will provide a space for students to participate. It makes good sense that the purposes of evaluation should be clear, give everyone (students, staff, parents, and community) involved an opportunity to participate and that anonymity is ensured to express honest opinions (Bennett, 1989).

What Is Evaluation?

So what is evaluation? Essentially, evaluation helps you to understand the effectiveness of instructional activities and programs.

It involves collecting data and analyzing information to better understand characteristics and outcomes so you can improve your programs, projects and initiatives (Patton, 1987). You want the evaluation process to be valid, reliable and of practical use. For evaluation to be valid, use well-defined criteria that are specific to the subject (e.g., sustainability). A reliable evaluation is consistent each time it is used, including across items (e.g., test questions). Finally, all evaluations should be realistic and practical. Using data from an evaluation is an excellent way to promote a successful program.

A wonderful tool that can be used for evaluation throughout a project is the Evaluation Toolbox (http://evaluationtoolbox.net.au/). This Australian website focuses on how to evaluate community sustainability projects. It is not focused specifically on PreK–12 schools, though much of the website is easily transferable to education. As teachers and administrators are not specifically trained in evaluation practices, it is certainly appropriate to seek expert assistance. This might not be possible due to a limited budget, and so this chapter and the Evaluation Toolbox website should be extremely helpful to complete the process on your own. Ultimately, you want to know what is working (or not working) in the sustainability projects you have created, and evaluation can help that effort. Also, an important part of the evaluation process is sharing your results with others. Without this type of communication, it is difficult to advance green schools to the next level.

If you are in a school that is considering developing green initiatives or applying for the ED-GRS (U.S. Green Ribbon) award, it might be helpful to contact your state education authority as they can send you the ED-GRS application (Green Ribbon State Contacts). The application will help you better understand the evaluation process and what is required. To get a better understanding of the Eco-School evaluation process, find your country on this map: https://www.ecoschools.global/national-offices/.

What Type of Evaluation Should Be Used?

Evaluation works best when it is built into the project from the beginning. It then becomes part of the project and an ongoing activity that people are used to doing. As it is typically helpful to see an example of a process, a case study will be discussed throughout this chapter so you can see how evaluation can be embedded into a project. **Reread the opening vignette at the beginning of the chapter.**

When starting a project, you will include formative evaluations that occur during program development and implementation. These evaluations will be useful in giving direction on how best to achieve your goals or improve the program. For example, a needs assessment will help with determining the need (or interest) for the project, who might need the project and how to go about meeting that need. As part of formative evaluation, you will want to understand how the project will be implemented and whether it is operating as planned (implementation evaluation). Understanding what resources are needed and if you have the capacity for the project are also important.

The garden at Roosevelt Middle School has been around for a while, and likely some of the teachers had started working at the school after the garden was established. They might not consider it an important factor in their own curriculum and so hadn't considered participating each year. Mrs. Willer convened a Green Team meeting to discuss some ideas. As she wanted to do a major revision of the garden, this would be a good time to include an evaluation process.

At the meeting, Mrs. Willer shared that she had some new ideas for the garden but wanted to get input from non-participating teachers before moving forward. The Green Team agreed, and a focus group was organized, including five randomly chosen teachers who had been working at Roosevelt less than ten years and didn't use the garden.

Summative evaluations will occur once you are well into your project and at the end of the project and can tell you whether you are achieving your goals. Outcome evaluation will look at the changes in program participants that are a direct result of the project. Summative evaluation is not about how many workshops are held or the number of people who attended a meeting (outputs) but are instead focused on how the workshops increased knowledge or skill or changed behavior (outcomes). An impact evaluation will look at the longer-term changes that may affect the entire school, community or the environment. Included in Table 9.1 are formative and summative project stages, evaluation questions, evaluation type and example evaluations. A number of example evaluations have hyperlinks, though if you are reading a hard copy of the book, you can go to: http://evaluationtoolbox.net. au/ to find all of the information in Table 9.1. Also, a number of the example evaluations can be used throughout the project, such as a project diary, storytelling, focus groups and interviews.

Another quality resource that supports environmental and sustainability evaluations is called My Environmental Education Evaluation Resource Assistant (MEERA), which has searchable environmental evaluations that you can use (https://meera.snre. umich.edu/search-evaluations). Click on the search terms you are interested in, and it will show you a sample evaluation that another school or organization has implemented. If you want to browse all of the included evaluations, click here: https://meera. snre.umich.edu/browse-evaluation.

Each type of evaluation in Table 9.1 is going to collect either quantitative or qualitative data. Quantitative data are going to help you better understand the "what" of your research question. These data will be in number form so can be counted or compared. For example, a Likert scale using a rating scale from 1 to 5 (strongly disagree to strongly agree) or the number of times teachers use the garden can be collected. Questionnaires are one way to collect quantitative data. Qualitative data will give you information about participant characteristics, such as the reasons why teachers use (or don't use) the garden. A focus group, observation or open-ended questions are ways to collect qualitative data. The data are descriptive words and patterns found from the notes taken or questions answered. For example, if you were to review the notes from the garden focus group (see next text box), you could review the interview notes to find themes or meaningful phrasing that will help you to identify participants ideas.

Evaluating the Interconnection of Sustainability Initiatives

For a school be a true green school, projects and initiatives should be interconnected across the curriculum, community and

TABLE 9.1 Project Evaluation Toolbox

PROJECT STAGE	Before Project Begins	New Project	Established Project	Mature Project	End of Project
EVALUATION QUESTIONS	Why are we doing this? What do we hope to accomplish? Is it a new project or refining an established project? Where will project occur? How much time and effort will be required to complete the project and evaluation? Are the appropriate people included?	Is the project operating as planned? Are intended participants involved?	Is the project achieving its objectives?	What predicted and unpredicted impacts has the program had?	To what extent did the project meet overall needs? What were the specific features of the project that made a difference? Has the project been cost-effective? Is the project the best use of time, energy, resources and funding?
EVALUATION TYPE	Needs assessment	Process evaluation	Implementation evaluation	Impact evaluation	Outcome evaluation
EXAMPLE EVALUATIONS	Problem/solution tree analysis Stakeholder analysis Project Diary (use throughout project) Outcome hierarchy	Footprint calculator (complete pre- and post)	Semi-structured interview Observation (can be used during project)	Focus group Questionnaire	Storytelling (can be used throughout project)

Adapted from Pancer and Westhues (1989), Rossi et al. (2004) and Evaluation Toolbox (2010).

At the focus group, the Green Team asked the five non-participating teachers to share their ideas about the garden and asked them if they would be interested in starting a new project that included the outdoor space. Mrs. Willer shared her ideas as well and developed a consensus on the next steps. During the hour-long meeting, one of the Green Team members took notes and then sent them out to everyone attending to make sure they were accurate. The Green Team met once more, including the administration, to get approval on the next steps. A proposal was sent out to school staff (including custodians, cafeteria workers, teachers and other school staff) so that everyone received an overview of the project. Proposal comments were requested and reviewed. Once comments were discussed with the Green Team members and the administration, the review proposal was fairly simple: the Green Team would like to create a makerspace that uses food and gardening as an opportunity for innovation.

campus (Elser et al., 2011). These three interconnected levels are defined as follows:

◆ Curriculum: projects focus on classroom activities, teacher/ student interaction, content and class programming, professional development and training, etc.
◆ Campus: projects relate to school and school district operation, which include staff and administration practices, physical facilities, school grounds and open space, operation and maintenance, etc.
◆ Community: projects focus on a school's wider influence and partnerships, including parent participation, collaboration with the business community, interaction with government and non-profits or NGOs (non-governmental organizations), etc. (Warner & Elser, 2015, p. 4).

Included in these interconnected levels are the health and wellness of teachers, students and staff, a healthy environment and economic efficiency (how resources are used). It is important that your school be connected to the local community so students are able to make connections between what they are learning and real-world experiences.

Most schools that are focused on "greening" their school emphasize environmental/campus initiatives such as recycling, energy conservation or gardens. Some of these projects are interconnected with other sustainability activities such as a math teacher focusing on monthly solar panel production compared to predicted yield. The more interconnected the sustainability initiatives, the stronger the projects and, hence, the greener the school. There are key features that characterize the highly interconnected nature of sustainability initiatives, which include the following:

- ◆ Incorporate an emphasis on interdisciplinary, problem-based learning into the school curriculum.
    - Students work across content areas to identify school/community sustainability issues and then work to find solutions.
- ◆ Numerous "contact points" between grade levels and disciplines and between disciplines and administrators – essentially more lines of communication – are open.
- ◆ The vision of the school emphasizes sustainability, and it permeates into the campus, community and curriculum.
- ◆ Each year there are more complex sustainability initiatives, with deeper emphasis, student control, experiential learning and problem-solving of real-world environmental problems (Warner & Elser, 2015).

One of the goals at Roosevelt was to improve students' interest and willingness to eat nutritional food. The Green Team felt that the culinary makerspace would encourage students to experiment with different types of food. Once the administration approved the idea, the Green Team canvased the underutilized spaces at the school to see where the makerspace might be appropriate. A supply space that was approximately 20 × 18 feet was little used and only required moving some cleaning materials to another room. The woodshop teacher at the high school was contacted and agreed to work with the Green Team on making some tables and butcher block for cutting ingredients. Teachers at Roosevelt sent notes home with students explaining the upcoming makerspace and asked for kitchen donations. Parents sent in mixing bowls, baking dishes and pans, utensils, measuring cups, dishes, bowls, flatware, etc. The Green Team submitted a grant through Lowe's, which has an education grant program, (www.toolboxforeducation.com) and received a cook top, oven and dishwasher. A used refrigerator was donated from a local company, and a large TV screen so students can view cooking videos was received through the donor's choose program (https://www.donorschoose.org/). From finding the room through setting up appliances and being ready for students to use, the culinary makerspace took about five months to set up.

CREDIT Pedro Felipe Linares, Colegio Los Nogales

In Photo 9.1, third grade students at Colegio Los Nogales are working on a compost inquiry project that integrates numerous content areas.

Now, let's consider a school that recycles but does not connect it to other school activities or curriculum. The person who started the recycling program leaves, and the coordination of how the recyclables are collected falls apart. If that school had integrated recycling into the curriculum and other school initiatives (see bulleted list), the strength of the program would be enough that if one teacher or staff member left, it would still continue.

- ◆ The school curriculum includes a recycling monitoring system that collects data on how much waste the school keeps out of the landfill.
- ◆ One grade level in the school incorporates a thematic unit on systems, which includes an investigation into trash. The unit would emphasize issues with trash, research

solutions and create motivational ideas on how to reduce trash.

◆ Have students create posters and give presentations to classes about the recycling program and how it works.

◆ Create a fund that supports recycling by getting refunds for old iPads, computers, iPhones, printing ink cartridges and soda cans.

◆ Use www.BookCrossing.com to swap books. Students (and teachers) register the book on the site and mark the inside cover with the URL and an ID# provided by the site. Then, the owner of the book can pass it along to someone else or leave it at a book-swap table. New readers are asked to join the site and post comments about the book.

See Figure 9.1 to get a better understanding of how a school could evaluate whether sustainability issues connect across campus, curriculum and community.

The Evaluation Process for Both Course- and Campus-Based Sustainability Initiatives

When thinking about how to evaluate sustainability initiatives, consider the end point of the project. Are you focused on a solution, an innovative product or an outcome? One way to evaluate these initiatives is to use the theoretical framework of "experiential learning," which emphasizes generating plausible solutions using existing knowledge.

Evaluation of Course-Based Sustainability Initiatives

Wouldn't it be an amazing experience to have students that hold themselves accountable towards achieving end results? This is a real possibility if there are clear outcome indicators, a use of formative assessment (including self-assessment) and a process for revision of work. Following these specific steps

FIGURE 9.1 Interconnectedness of sustainability initiatives

CREDIT Linda H. Plevyak, PhD

will help to make the evaluation process more successful and student driven:

1. Learning-appropriate goals.
2. Scaffolds that support both student and teacher learning.
3. Frequent opportunities for formative self-assessment and revision.
4. Social organizations that promote participation and result in a sense of agency (Barron et al., 1998, p. 273).

First, including learning-appropriate goals helps students understand the how and why of a project. For example, if the goal of the project is to create a recipe using items from the garden, the students will need to know the characteristics of a good recipe, including ingredients, measurements, step-by-step directions, etc. They will also need to understand how to evaluate the prepared food, considering the balance and contrast of the different flavors (salty, sour, sweet, etc.) and textures (crunchy, smooth, etc.). Having driving questions that foster focused inquiry will support the evaluation process. In relation to the garden recipe, the driving question might be, how can ingredients be put together to create a flavorful taste that has the right texture? As part of the formative assessment, have the students generate their own questions to guide their investigation. An exit ticket or random brief interviews with students will help you to know if the students understood the learning goal.

Second, using scaffolds can "help students and teachers continually reflect on how and why their current activities are relevant to the overall goals (the big picture) of the project" (Barron et al., 1998, p. 277). Scaffolds can include embedded teaching, which essentially means "learning by doing" or instructing during activities when students are more engaged and interested in the experience. Another example of scaffolding is providing students with a problem-based learning experience prior to conducting their own projects, which will create higher-quality work (Barron et al., 1998). The problem-based scenario could be a simulated problem-based experience that helps students see the complexity and innuendo of the project experience. The simulation can also be over a short period – for instance, three or four one-hour class periods. This understanding of how a problem can be solved and what to look for can help students delve deeper into their own projects and can help provide scaffolding during the evaluation process.

Third, setting up formative assessment prior to implementing a project can help students reflect and be aware of particular features and ideas. For example, have the students analyze the differences between two or more examples. If you are discussing rivers, you can provide two different tools and have the students compare them as to which would be a better tool for testing water quality. Comparing and contrasting the tools will help them develop questions about the testing process, what is needed and how to best go about it.

In a classroom that emphasizes projects and problem-based learning, the cycle of establishing goals and questions, scaffolding concepts, frequent formative assessment and communication will naturally lend itself to revision. Student-generated products can be reviewed by peers, groups, a teacher or outside professionals. Students can use the feedback to revise designs and plans. For example, if the teacher is providing feedback, it should be fairly general and help the students rethink concepts while providing resources they can consult for further information. Teachers should check back as the revision process occurs to make sure enough scaffolds are in place for the students to be successful with the revision process. Including a feedback sheet or rubric that includes criteria and project questions can help focus students on important items. Providing general feedback (with the feedback sheet or rubric) supports an important instructional goal of helping students to become lifelong learners. Students should see the learning process as something that they will continue, even outside of the classroom.

Lastly, social organizations can transition students from being passive to actively engaging with materials, other students, the teacher, etc. Included in project-based learning should be opportunities for small-group discussions, peer review and reviewing how others have thought about the same problem the students are working on. Connecting to outside groups to discuss and present ideas can provide a meaningful experience for students as well as offer a new way to learn and communicate with others.

Evaluation of Campus-Based Sustainability Initiatives

Creating an evaluation plan for campus sustainability initiatives will help you better understand what is and is not working. First, establish consensus on the project and the required steps that will be taken to implement it. Next, create the evaluation plan by framing questions that will help you to know the effectiveness of the sustainability initiative. Implementing the evaluation as part of the project includes collecting data, analyzing and interpreting the results and taking action on the findings and recommendations. For example, if you are interested in understanding whether conducting a project in the garden helps students deepen their relationship with nature, you could measure their connection with nature before they start work (pretest) and after they finish the project (posttest) and compare the scores (Salazar et al., 2020). There are numerous other evaluation designs that can be used to answer evaluation questions – for example, posttest only or two groups (control and experimental groups), which could use random or non-random groups. Also keep in mind that a short field trip is likely to not be impactful, and doing a pre- and post-analysis will not allow you to see much of a change. A minimum time to see a difference in knowledge, skill or attitude is a time commitment of two to three hours per day for a week or more.

An evaluation plan will need to include learning-appropriate goals (see previous section on course-based sustainability initiatives for more information). These learning-appropriate goals could be assessed using self-reflection, exit surveys, portfolio assessment or rubrics (Peppler et al., 2017). For example, Table 9.2 shares an example rubric for the Roosevelt case study. Keep in mind that students should receive the evaluation criteria at the beginning of a project.

Creating a timeline of the project and evaluation process will be helpful in keeping track of important goals and activities such as creating a survey, monitoring activity and evaluating results.

When collecting, analyzing and interpreting data, you have to be careful to make sure that bias is not part of the evaluation process (consciously or unconsciously). You can't avoid all bias, but you can try and prevent it as much as possible. For example, in the Roosevelt focus group, the teachers were randomly chosen, which helps to eliminate

> Table 9.2 is a rubric that will be used by the Roosevelt Green Team at the end of the spring quarter (spring 2023) to better understand how the teachers used the garden and the culinary makerspace. It can be part of the semistructured interviews or used as part of a teacher survey.

TABLE 9.2 Example rubric for the Roosevelt case study

	Novice	*Emergent*	*Leader*
Understanding of sustainability	Limited view of sustainability with little connection or understanding of the economic, social or equity issues with the environment.	Makes some connections to the environment and understands some of the concepts of sustainability that might include economic, social or equity.	Transformational view of sustainability that includes acting with integrity and responsibility in caring for the environment. Considers the economic, social and equity dimensions of sustainability.
Application of sustainability	Is limited in understanding how to take action in relation to the environment. Has difficulty articulating how they might be able to take steps to positively impact sustainability issues.	Has some understanding of how to take action in relation to the environment. Is able to articulate some ways that sustainability issues can be positively impacted.	Is able to provide numerous actionable items in relation to the environment. Provides quality examples and steps to take in how sustainability issues could be positively impacted.
Amount of time spent on sustainability issues	Spends less than 30 minutes a week on the environment, going outside or incorporating sustainability concepts into courses.	Spends between 30 minutes and 2 hours per week on the environment, going outside or incorporating sustainability concepts into courses.	Spends more than two hours per week on the environment, going outside or incorporating sustainability concepts into courses.
Ethics	Does not engage or consider ethics in relation to the environment.	Some informal discussion about ethics in relation to the environment. Though does not go in depth with values or beliefs about sustainability.	Deeply considers and applies personal, social and civic values in relation to sustainability. Goes in depth on multiple ethical perspectives.

	Novice	*Emergent*	*Leader*
Experiential or service learning	Emphasizes lecture and comprehension with little opportunity for service. Conducts environmental activities that "help" the environment, but not their place in it.	Some interactive learning with engagement in authentic experiences, including debrief and analysis. Some opportunities for service and action towards the environment with authentic interaction with peers, the schools, community, or larger world.	In-depth service that includes critical, reflective thinking and civic responsibility. Student-led inquiry that focus on community investigations. Significant opportunities for students to make decisions, plan, execute, monitor and evaluate their ideas and actions.

Adapted from: Creative Change Education Solutions (2014).

selection bias. If a questionnaire is going to be used, the following points will help to reduce response bias:

♦ Answer options should not be leading.
♦ Allow participants to remain anonymous.
♦ Neutrally word questions.
♦ Have the front office distribute the questionnaire so it isn't obvious who is requesting the information.
♦ Keep questions short and clear.

Table 9.3 shares an example timeline for the Roosevelt Garden Project that includes both project and evaluation goals. The Green Team (project team) creates the goals, objectives, activities, timeline and person responsible so that everyone has a sense of how the project will be completed. The plan may need to be revised due to changing circumstances.

Grant Writing and Funding

Grant funds are available for numerous sustainable projects (see resource list at the end of the book for grant ideas). Be sure to

TABLE 9.3 Example timeline for the Roosevelt Garden Project

Project (P) and Evaluation (E)	Goals	Related Objective	Activity	Expected Completion Date	Person(s) Responsible
E	Gain an understanding of teacher needs in relation to garden.	Complete data collection for focus group.	Conduct a focus group with five randomly chosen teachers.	April 2020	Mrs. Willer and two Green Team members
P	Create a culinary makerspace with requisite supplies that are near the outdoor garden.	Include kitchen supplies, access to water and cooking supplies, tables, appliances, etc.	Work with administration to use a space near the garden for the culinary makerspace.	April–August 2020	Green Team
E	Establish a proposal and send to all Roosevelt staff and teachers.	Receive feedback about the proposal.	Submit proposal to all staff and teachers, request comments, review and revise proposal.	May 2020	Mrs. Willer, Green Team and principal
P	Have all teachers complete the garden and makerspace training video with their students.	Monitor who has completed training.	Create a brief training video and guide for teachers and students to complete prior to using garden and makerspace.	End of the first school quarter (fall 2020)	Tech coordinator and Green Team
E	Have at least 80% of teachers actively using the garden.	Monitor the garden and makerspace for number of teachers and students.	Create a brief reservation portal that teachers use to reserve garden and makerspace.	Throughout spring quarter (spring 2021)	Mrs. Willer

P	*Increase momentum and excitement with inventing new recipes and experimenting with different fruits and vegetables.*	*Support a marketing campaign that shares information and creates interest.*	*Create PR campaign that uses social media, posters, personal communication and email.*	*Throughout spring quarter (spring 2021)*	*Green Team*
E	*Gain an understanding of quality garden and makerspace experiences.*	*Monitor types of learning, skills and attitudes of teachers and students.*	*Conduct a semistructured interview with randomly chosen teachers and students who participated and did not participate in garden and makerspace experiences.*	*End of the spring quarter (spring 2021)*	*Green Team*

talk with your school district central office as they may have someone that can help with grant writing. It is also a good idea to get administration approval prior to submitting the grant proposal. For grants over $5,000, you may even need school board approval. Typically, you will submit for a small grant ($500 or less) prior to going for larger grants. You can also find example grant proposals on the grant funder's website or contact them for a sample of their winning grants. If you have received a grant, you will need someone to track the money that is spent on the project. Using an Excel spreadsheet is likely the easiest way to track actual cost. Keeping notes on the spreadsheet is helpful to explain differences between what you projected to spend versus what was actually spent. These notes will also help in lessons learned and provide a guide for your next project.

The feedback from the random semistructured interviews (using the rubric in Table 9.3) at the end of spring 2021 showed that both teachers and students fit into either the emergent or leader columns in relation to understanding sustainability. Students were also applying sustainability concepts to the garden and engaging in the makerspace by making recipes. The use of the garden by classes had increased by 25%, and the makerspace schedule was filled at least 50% each week. The goal for the next academic year was to expand the makerspace to include a greenhouse with solar panels. One of the school board members had found a potential grant at http://schoolgreenhouses.com/. A few of the teachers had also suggested getting a 3D printer so that students could create gardening tools or appliance parts. Another suggestion was to get materials for solar food dryers to dry and preserve fruits and vegetables. Based on the feedback and suggestions, the Green Team were excited that there was so much interest and participation in the garden and culinary makerspace!

Evaluation of Community Relationships to Keep Them Healthy and Meaningful

Developing relationships with outside organizations is a wonderful way to include different perspectives in a green school. These relationships also provide access to experts, guest speakers, evaluators and a support network that can help with course- and campus-based sustainability initiatives. Including a memorandum of understanding (MOU) between the school and the partner organization will help to keep track of a common vision, mutually agreed upon expectations and project goals. It is not a legally binding agreement but will help to solidify the partnership and keep both groups on course.

These relationships can include a wide variety of organizations, including other schools, the parent-teacher association (PTA), businesses, non-profit organizations, government offices, recreation centers, parks, museums and art institutions. The more diversity in your outside relationships, the more real world experiences the students can have both on and off campus. As you want students to engage with experiential, reflective learning, you want to establish parameters with outside groups so they understand expectations. For example, when preparing guests to come to class, you want to make sure they know the goals for the interaction. Do you want them to conduct a demonstration, give a lecture about native plants or work with the students about designing a nature trail on school property?

Establishing a good system of communication will go far in making sure that everyone in and outside of the school feels comfortable with the relationship. Recognizing different viewpoints and getting more voices in a conversation will strengthen the bond among group members. In this type of climate, "there is a willingness to learn from the experiences, viewpoints and arguments of others" (Verhelst et al., 2020, p. 408). You may want to include a dedicated physical space in the school where volunteers or members of outside organizations can meet with teachers and staff. If a dedicated space isn't possible, meetings could take place in a classroom, teacher's lounge, library, cafeteria or some other unused space. It is important that outside groups feel welcome and appreciated. You might have students conduct school tours so that groups can get a sense of the school and sustainability initiatives. The more the students are engaged with outside organizations, the more a sense of community can be developed.

There are some community members, such as retired teachers or gardeners, who might be interested in volunteering to help with planting, weeding and watering the garden. Consider who

188 ◆ Teaching Towards Green Schools

will set up the weekly schedule, and make sure appropriate tools are available and that volunteers know the process for signing in and finding their way around campus. Coordinating volunteers is important and could be a teacher who oversees the garden or a parent volunteer who knows the school system. At least once a year, all school volunteers (and the teachers and staff that interact with them) should be asked to complete a survey on their perceptions of what is and is not working and what improvements could be made. It can be a fairly simple survey with a Likert scale (strongly agree, agree, disagree, strongly disagree) for responses and short answer questions.

Have either the Green Team or another group review survey data. Random interviews of outside group members and internal teachers and staff that actively engage with them might also be a helpful way to better understand how the school/organization relationship is going. If there is more than one organization involved in the school, be sure to separate data based on the different groups. Analyze the data for concerning areas such as respondents not feeling like they are productive or wanted while at the school. Sit down with outside group members to discuss the data, and revise the MOU and/or goals in concert with results, interviews and discussions. Having a recognition lunch for those who participate on the Green Team, volunteers, teachers and staff that support sustainability initiatives will be greatly appreciated and go a long way in having everyone continue their efforts year after year!

Conclusions

Evaluation is an important part of curriculum, campus and community sustainability initiatives. It can help with understanding what students are learning and the effectiveness of a sustainability project. Evaluations, such as surveys or interview questions, should include short and clear language. Once the data have been collected, it should be analyzed so that you understand if you are meeting project outcomes. Both formative (used during the implementation process) and summative evaluation (at the end of the project) can be used to see whether you are achieving your goals. The interconnection of sustainability initiatives across grades, content areas, campus and community can be created through increased contact points (across grades and content areas and among student, staff, teachers and community) to promote more communication, interdisciplinary curriculum and more complex sustainability initiatives each year. Including outside organizations in a green school can provide access to numerous individuals that can support your projects. Open communication is key, and including a yearly survey of all those involved will help to understand what is and is not working.

Questions to Consider

- ◆ What projects or initiatives are you considering implementing?
- ◆ After reviewing this chapter, what type of evaluation will help you to understand if you have achieved your goals?
- ◆ Do you work with outside organizations? If so, do you evaluate the relationship? If not, what organization can you connect with to support a sustainability initiative?

References

Barron, B. J., Schwartz, D. L., Vye, N. J., Moore, A., Petrosino, A., Zech, L., & Bransford, J. D. (1998). Doing with understanding: Lessons from research on problem- and project-based learning. *The Journal of the Learning Sciences, 7*(3–4), 271–311.

Bennett, D. B. (1989). *Evaluating environmental education in schools: A practical guide for teachers.* UNESCO.

Creative Change Education Solutions. (2014). *Integrating sustainability across the curriculum: Disciplinary connections and rubrics.* Integration of Sustainability into the Curriculum.

Elser, M. M., Pollari, L., Frisk, E., & Wood, M. W. (2011). Linking curriculum and learning to facilities: Arizona State University's GK–12 sustainable schools program. *Educational Facility Planner, 45*(3), 7–10.

Evaluation Toolbox. (2010). *Community sustainability engagement*. http:// evaluationtoolbox.net.au/.

Nelson, G. (n.d.). http://www.nelsonearthday.net/nelson/.

Pancer, S. M., & Westhues, A. (1989). A developmental stage approach to program planning and evaluation. *Evaluation Review, 13*(1), 56–77.

Patton, M. Q. (1987). *Qualitative research evaluation methods*. Sage Publications.

Peppler, K., Keune, A., Xia, F., & Chang, S. (2017). *Makerspace assessment*. Survey of Assessment in Makerspaces.

Rossi, R. H., Lipsey, M. W., & Freeman, H. E. (2004). *Evaluation: A systematic approach*. Sage Publications.

Salazar, G., Kunkle, K., & Monroe, M. C. (2020). *Practitioner guide to assessing connection to nature*. North American Association for Environmental Education.

Stokking, K., van Aert, L., Meijberg, W., & Kaskens, A. (1999). *Evaluating environmental education*. The World Conservation Union.

Verhelst, D., Vanhoof, J., Boeve-de Pauw, J., & Van Petegem, P. (2020). Building a conceptual framework for an ESD-effective school organization. *The Journal of Environmental Education, 51*(6), 400–415.

Warner, B. P., & Elser, M. (2015). How do sustainable schools integrate sustainability education? An assessment of certified sustainable K–12 schools in the United States. *Journal of Environmental Education, 46*(1), 1–22.

Additional Resources

Curriculum

Environmental Books
https://www.huffpost.com/entry/childrens-books-environment_l_5d6
6f45de4b063c341fa409c
This is a good list of books that teach kids about the environment.

Cleaner and Greener (Energy Efficiency and Renewable Energy)
http://cleanerandgreener.org/resources.html
Emissions and emissions-reduction calculators.

Climate Generation
https://www.climategen.org/our-core-programs/climate-change-
education/curriculum/
Grades 3–12 curricula that focus on green careers, renewable energy
and climate change.

Contributing to Education Through Digital Access to Research (CEDAR)
https://cedar.wwu.edu/ftfcurriculum/
Field-tested curriculum guides for literacy, language arts, math, social
studies and science.

Green Schools Travel Program
https://www.nationaltransport.ie/wp-content/uploads/2019/09/NTA-
Toolkit-for-School-Travel-Final.pdf
This includes a toolkit developed in Ireland to decrease car and bus
trips while increasing walking and biking to and from school. Also
includes a number of resources and brief descriptions of activities
for a number of content areas.

Green Teacher Magazine
https://greenteacher.com/
Quarterly magazine that highlights curriculum articles, case studies,
resource lists, etc.

K–12 Environmental Education: Guidelines for Excellence
https://naaee.org/eepro/publication/excellence-environmental-
    education-guidelines-learning-k-12
A roadmap to achieving environmental literacy by setting expectations
    for fourth (age 10), eighth (age 14) and twelfth grade (age 18)
    students and outlining a framework for effective and comprehen-
    sive environmental education programs and curricula.

Makerspace Guidebook
https://makered.org/wp-content/uploads/2014/09/Makerspace-
    Playbook-Feb-2013.pdf
This makerspace guide will help to understand how to create a
    makerspace.

Recycle Rally
https://pepsicorecycling.com/RecycleRally
Has resources and tools to help with recycling.

Renewable Energy Curriculum for High School
https://www.nrel.gov/docs/gen/fy01/30926.pdf
PDF file of various high school research projects that focus on renew-
    able energy.

Solar Energy International
https://www.solarenergy.org/solar-in-the-schools/
Solar in the Schools teaches about the different types of renewable
    energy, basic electricity and solar photovoltaics using online cur-
    riculum and in-person experiential learning for K–12.

Solar Panel Simulation
https://mitsloan.mit.edu/teaching-resources-library/eclipsing-com
    petition-solar-pv-industry-simulation
Technology or economics teachers could have their classes complete
    the Solar PV Industry Simulation that highlights competition with
    the solar panel industry.

Teaching Green: The Elementary Years
https://greenteacher.com/
Book that includes environmental education lessons for elementary
    education.

Teaching Green: The Middle School Years
https://greenteacher.com/
Book that includes environmental education lessons for middle school.

Teaching Green: The High School Years
https://greenteacher.com/
Book that includes environmental education lessons for high school.

Teaching Teens About Climate Change
https://greenteacher.com/product/teaching-teens-about-climate-
    change-ebook/
Book written in 2017 that focuses on increasing students' understanding
    of the impacts of climate change, learning about carbon-regulation
    strategies such as carbon taxes and cap and trade and exploring
    options for sustainable transportation. Costs $10.99 on the www.
    greenteacher.com site.

U.S. Energy Information Administration
www.eia.doe.gov
Website for kids with renewable energy basics.

U.S. Green Building Council
https://www.usgbc.org/leed
LEED certification information for schools interested in redesign of K–12
    buildings.

U.S. National Energy Education Development
https://www.need.org/
Includes curricula that correlates to the National Science Education
    Standards for all grade levels and all U.S. states.

World Wildlife Federation (2021).
https://www.nwf.org/Eco-Schools-USA/Pathways/Audit.
Environmental audits for K–2, 3–5, 6–8 and 9–12 that include energy,
    water, transportation, schoolyard habitats, healthy living, etc.

Evaluation

Evaluating Your Environmental Education Program
https://naaee.org/eepro/publication/evaluating-your-environ
    mental-education

This is a workbook that helps you design and conduct an evaluation through exercises, case studies and examples. Cost: $25.

Evaluation Toolbox
http://evaluationtoolbox.net.au/
This website will help with sustainability evaluation projects and provides great examples.

Practitioner Guide to Assessing a Connection to Nature
NAAEE Guide
This is a very helpful guide that shares rubrics, interview questions, scales and other evaluation tools.

Grants

Bullitt Foundation
https://www.bullitt.org/
Organization that gives grants for energy, green buildings, environmental fellowships, etc.

Canadian Climate Change Connection
https://climatechangeconnection.org/resources/climate-friendly-schools/youth-funding/
Shares links to various environmental funding sources.

Clean Energy Resource Teams (CERT)
https://www.cleanenergyresourceteams.org/
Offers support to schools in Minnesota with technical advice, funding, tools and resources.

Doris Duke Foundation
https://www.rwjf.org/en/library/funding-opportunities/2021/people-parks-and-power-a-national-initiative-for-green-space-health-equity-and-racial-justice.html
Grants that can go up to $500,000 (over two years) for low-income urban schools.

Environmental Protection Agency
https://www.epa.gov/education/grants

Grants for environmental education projects that design, demonstrate and/or disseminate environmental education practices, methods or techniques.

Finding Grant Funding
https://peacefulplaygrounds.com/getting-your-school-grant-funded/
This website helps understand the grant-funding process.

Gray Family Foundation
https://grayff.org/grants/environmental-education/
Supports environmental education teaching.

National Environmental Education Fund (NEEF)
https://www.neefusa.org/grants
Supports communities who are interested in improving the environment.

North American Association for Environmental Education
https://naaee.org/eepro/opportunities
Various grants and awards that support environmental improvement and environmental education.

Pisces Foundation
https://piscesfoundation.org/rfp/
Environmental and outdoor learning grants.

Walmart Foundation
https://fconline.foundationcenter.org/fdo-grantmaker-profile?
key=WALM001
Walmart foundation funds sustainability projects.

Green Cleaning Product Information

Edutopia: Green Cleaning Products Guide
https://www.edutopia.org/green-schools-environment-products-cleaning
Explains how to choose environmentally safe cleaning products.

EPA: Safer Choice
https://www.epa.gov/saferchoice

This website shares information about the products that have earned the EPA EcoLogo.

Green Schools Initiative
http://www.greenschools.net/display.php-modin=54&uid=56.html
Shares information about green cleaning products and how they received EcoLogo and Green Seal certification.

Health and Wellness

Safe Routes to School
http://www.saferoutesinfo.org/
The National Center for Safe Routes to School (NCSR) helps schools create safe routes to school.

Walk or Bike to School
http://www.walkbiketoschool.org/
This website helps to plan a walk or bike school event.

Policy Development and Collaboration to Support Sustainability

Educators for Excellence
https://e4e.org/
Supporting a teacher voice in educational policy decisions.

Green Schools Alliance (GSA)
https://www.greenschoolsalliance.org
The GSA is a non-profit organization that promotes collaboration between school districts to support a greener, more efficient process to purchasing, curriculum development and sustainable solutions.

Hope Street Group
https://hopestreetgroup.org/
Advocate economic opportunity for all Americans.

List of Non-Profits that Support Sustainable Practices
https://teachersinspired.com/become-a-green-school-here-are-8-
    organizations-ready-to-help/
https://greatnonprofits.org/categories/view/environmental-education
https://naaee.org/our-partners/nonprofits
https://www.aashe.org/partners/association-nonprofit-partners/
https://www.healthygreenschools.org/about/participating-
    organizations/
There are numerous non-profit organizations that support sustainability
    practices.

Teach Plus
https://teachplus.org/
Empower teachers to provide leadership in advocating educational policy.

Professional Development/Teacher Support

Australian Education for Sustainability Alliance
https://sustainabilityinschools.edu.au/
Website that has high-quality education resources, case studies focused
    on how to create change and information on how to link it all back
    to the curriculum – in an accessible, direct way.

Benefits of Environmental Education for K–12 Students
https://naaee.org/eepro/research/eeworks/student-outcomes
Case studies, research and key findings as to how to effectively imple-
    ment environmental education.

Center for Green Schools
https://www.centerforgreenschools.org/resources
Numerous resources that highlight policy and legislation, LEED certifica-
    tion, and COVID-19 air-quality information.

Green Schools National Network
https://greenschoolsnationalnetwork.org/
Focuses on best practices in leadership, curriculum and instruction, cul-
    ture and climate and facilities and operations.

NAAEE affiliate organizations
https://naaee.org/our-partners/affiliates
These organizations focus on state and local environmental education.

Online Platform for the K–12 EE Community
https://naaee.org/eepro/groups/k-12-ee.
Join this group to get questions answered, find teacher resources for
the classroom, take action and join the conversation for a greener,
brighter future!

Online Platform for the Higher Education EE Community
https://naaee.org/eepro/groups/higher-education
This group focuses on undergraduate, graduate and green-campus
ideas.